Perfection is not what it seems; in fact, it is just the opposite. In *The Perfection Paradox*, Jeffrey A. Kramer uses a lifetime of examples to paint a clear and powerful picture of the damaging impacts of perfectionism on work and life. Fortunately for him, and for us, he also shares simple and actionable steps to escape from the prison of perfection.

—**Dr. Marshall Goldsmith**, *New York Times* bestselling author of *What Got You Here Won't Get You There* and *Triggers*, World's #1 Executive Coach, and *Harvard Business Review*'s World's #1 Leadership Thinker

Perfectionism seems to be not so much a desire for excellence as it is the fear of inadequacy showing up as procrastination. In *The Perfection Paradox,* Jeff uses his own experiences to guide us from hiding behind perfectionism to the freedom of a life that is rich with meaningful accomplishments and relationships.

—**Dan Miller**, *New York Times* bestselling author of *48 Days to the Work You Love,* and host of the 48 Days Podcast

Who would have thought that perfection could actually prevent excellence by inducing a paralyzing fear of failure, and creating a habit of negativity, distraction and procrastination? Indeed, that is the contradiction Jeffrey A. Kramer explores in his book *The Perfection Paradox*. If you are finding that being a perfectionist has its dark side, this book can help you explore and conquer the harmful side of perfect and find a rewarding path to excellence for yourself and those around you.

—**Elizabeth McCormick**, former US Army Black Hawk Pilot, #5 on the list of Leadership Experts to follow online, author of *The PILOT Method*

Perfection is far from the good thing it masquerades as. In *The Perfection Paradox*, Jeff shows us how it's possible to recognize and escape from this crippling deception. He provides a proven process to find clarity and experience a life of freedom.
—**Kary Oberbrunner**, CEO of Igniting Souls, author of *Unhackable*

If you are a fellow perfectionist who puts off until tomorrow what you should have done yesterday, *The Perfection Paradox* is a must-read. Jeff leads the reader through the maze of analysis paralysis, fear of failure, dealing with distraction, and escaping the addiction to the realization that imperfect action beats perfect inaction every time! For myself, learning to take imperfect action was a game-changer, and it can be for you too!
—**Lisa Moser**, Author/Coach/Speaker, www.LisaMoser.com

How do we enjoy the benefits of perfectionism without the negative side effects? It's a question so many of us struggle with. Jeff's book provides a practical, realistic pathway to get there—to "live inside the paradox."
—**Jerod Morris**, Chief Creative Thinker for THINKERS Notebook

If seeking perfection or rather using it as an excuse has stalled you in the past, here is your permission to get over it. *The Perfection Paradox* provides simple steps to break the cycle of seeking the unattainable. To quote the author, "sometimes good is good enough". Enjoy the freedom you'll glean from this growth tool by letting go in order to experience authentic, satisfying and sustainable success.
—**Daphne V. Smith**, author of *What's YOUR Scarlet Letter?*, Chain Breaker and Wave Maker

Great read! This book does what all great books do. It makes you want to turn the page. As a recovering perfectionist, I have many years of recovery behind me. However, Jeff's heartfelt, transparent message raised my awareness relative to some things I still needed to address. As a result, I took immediate action and made a few adjustments that brought me a bit more internal peace. Thank you, sir!

—**Mack Story**, Leadership Speaker and Trainer, author of the Blue-Collar Leadership® Series

If you're delaying going after your big dream because you never have enough time, you're worried you might do it wrong or you're afraid of what others might say or think about you if you fail (or succeed), *The Perfection Paradox* is a must-read. By sharing his own story, Jeff reveals how perfectionism actually keeps you from reaching your goals, and breaks down how to dismantle perfectionism so that you accomplish anything.

—**Shannon Mattern**, host of the Pep Talks for Side Hustlers Podcast, mentor to side-hustling entrepreneurs who are building businesses online

Whether others have labeled you as a 'perfectionist' or you've secretly wondered yourself, pick up this book and you'll have an answer quickly! Kramer authentically reveals his personal experiences with perfectionism while incorporating a massive amount of intriguing stories and research. You won't be able to put down *The Perfect Paradox* and, as a result, you will finally know how to be 'good enough' on the other side of these pages.

—**Renee Vidor**, speaker, coach, and author of *Measuring Up: How to WIN in a World of Comparison*

Jeff's transparent expose' of his lifetime struggle with perfectionism sets the perfect stage for understanding the damage perfection causes, and the benefit of moving from perfect to letting good be good enough. Jeff has clearly shown the irony in the perfection paradox and that perfection is more a prison to escape from than an elusive paradise to be sought after. He has looked deep within and without in hopes of finding the sacred oasis, only to discover that what he was chasing was a mirage. That what he desired and needed most started the moment he took himself off the autobahn of perfection and started walking the open roads of good enough truly is good enough.

—**Martyn J. Wood**, The Stratospheric Life Coach

Jeff knows first-hand how attractive perfection seems to be, hiding itself as a virtue to seek. In his personal account of fear, shame and deception, Jeff shows the damaging impacts of this hidden addiction to ideal, followed by the simple steps to escape it and find a life truly worth living. The strength shown by Jeff is extraordinary, and it is empowering to see it evidenced on every page.

—**Kelly Schwab**, City Attorney for City of Chandler, AZ

Self-awareness is key to our success in life, and a large part of that is being aware of how we hold ourselves back. Jeff's book, *The Perfection Paradox*, helps you realize how you may be holding yourself back by setting an impossible standard of perfection for yourself and for others, causing procrastination, decreasing productivity, and rupturing relationships. Jeff reminds us that, "imperfect action is better than perfect inaction." This was a great read! Thanks, Jeff!

—**Ria Story**, author of *Fearfully and Wonderfully Me*

By reading *The Perfection Paradox* by Jeffrey A. Kramer, you learn about the importance of acting now, that the best moment is now and not tomorrow or the day after tomorrow.

—**Alfousseni Sidibe**, Founder of Live Your Dream Mali

The Perfection Paradox allows everyone to recognize themselves somewhere in this book. Jeff distills the struggles with perfection that prevent even the most talented person from realizing their full potential. This book is thought-provoking, insightful and rich with ideas.

—**Laura Dillingham**, Executive Strategic Partner at HPISolutions

THE
PERFECTION
PARADOX

Krista,

Be freed by your flaws and Escape to Excellence!

[signature]

THE PERFECTION PARADOX

ACCEPT YOUR ADDICTION,
OVERCOME YOUR OBSESSION, AND
ESCAPE TO EXCELLENCE

JEFFREY A. KRAMER

Published by Author Academy Elite
PO Box 43, Powell, OH 43035
www.AuthorAcademyElite.com

Library of Congress Cataloging: 2020918192

Paperback ISBN: 978-1-64746-524-7
Hardcover ISBN: 978-1-64746-525-4
E-book ISBN: 978-1-64746-526-1

Available in paperback, hardcover, e-book, and audiobook

All quotations, unless otherwise attributed, are from BrainyQuote,
https://www.brainyquote.com

To protect the privacy of those who appear in stories shared by the author, some details and names may have been changed. Any Internet addresses (websites, blogs, etc.) or contact information printed in this book are offered as a resource. They are not intended in any way to be or imply an endorsement by Author Academy Elite, nor does Author Academy Elite vouch for the content of these sites or information for the life of this book.

For Sharon
My wife, my best friend, and the greatest
partner a person could ever hope for.
Thank you for supporting and encouraging me,
and for putting up with years of perfectionism
at its worst. Perfection may not be attainable,
but I got as close as God allows with you!

And for Kary Oberbrunner
My coach, mentor, publisher, and friend.
Thank you for believing in me long before I did.

I am careful not to confuse excellence with perfection.
Excellence I can reach for; perfection is God's business.

— Michael J. Fox

CONTENTS

PART 3: PROGRESS—GETTING TO GOOD ENOUGH

APPENDICES

FOREWORD

At its very best, life can be difficult. But worse still, life can be even more challenging if one's ultimate goal is perfection. Mounting pressures in the endless pursuit of perfection can be unimaginable, unrelenting, and unbearable.

Let's face it; current societal issues don't make dealing with lack of perfection any easier. Instagram models displaying enviable physiques, luxuriating in exotic locales, cause us to yearn for that perfect lifestyle. Former classmates and colleagues posting celebration pictures of their new perfect dream jobs cause us to question our own work-a-day existence. Even friends and family members contribute to the problem by sharing photos of perfect babies, perfect parties, perfect hairstyles, even perfect meals. It can all be too much.

Life isn't perfect. It never has been, and it never will be. Despite the temptation to measure up to someone else's image of perfection, in one way or another, we are bound to fall short. Worse still, the desperate—and futile—pursuit of perfection ends up costing us more than we should ever be willing to pay. For too many intelligent, highly educated, hardworking, talented individuals, the mirage of perfection creates distractions, disorientation and disillusionment. That's why this book, Jeffrey A. Kramer's, *The Perfection Paradox,* is so critical.

I met Jeff more than 20 years ago. Our work and careers brought us together numerous times over the years in various conference and training settings. Without fail, Jeff was always well prepared, busy attending to details and working hard to deliver more than was promised or expected. I saw what others saw—a consummate professional at work. But I was blind to Jeff's staggering, even debilitating, obsession with perfection—an obsession courageously revealed and now, thankfully, rejected.

By way of Jeff's unusual vulnerability and real-life stories of struggle, we learn from his trials and tribulations. We come to realize how easy it can be to fall prey to the seductive embrace of perfection and the psychological deception that follows. But Jeff goes further still. He reveals the damaging effects of perfection on ourselves and others, and shows us simple, yet powerful steps available to overcome perfection's stranglehold.

One of the things I've come to know and appreciate about Jeff is his desire to serve and help others is unwavering. *The Perfection Paradox* does just that. This book serves to help others who might also suffer from an addiction to perfection, a means of escape.

As Jeff writes in the book, "imperfect action beats perfect inaction every day." Imperfect or not, I hope you take action, read on and benefit from the journey contained in these pages.

—Phillip Van Hooser, MBA, CSP, CPAE
Award-Winning Keynote Speaker; Leadership Trainer;
author of *Leaders Ought to Know: 11 Ground Rules for Common Sense Leadership*

INTRODUCTION

Perfection. It sounds appealing; after all, what's better than perfect? That's what I always believed, and it served me well for many years. At least I thought it had. What I didn't know at the time was I had fallen prey to an addiction I never knew existed, an addiction to The Ideal.

This addiction starts as a seemingly innocent desire to do great things. A perfectionist believes they are doing amazing work, are continuously approaching excellence in everything they do, and are helping others do the same. The problem is others don't see it through the same lens. When someone else looks at a perfectionist, they may see a procrastinator, a pessimist, someone who is inflexible and intolerant, or maybe a quitter. At least that's what has happened in my life.

I was the consummate overachiever but was always disappointed in what I viewed as my underachieving results. Everything I did needed to be the best, most complete, most efficient, most thorough, and on and on and on. You know the type. I needed to win to show how great I was. In each instance, I thought I was chasing excellence, but others saw me as a bad sport, a pessimist, anal-retentive, or just a jerk. I was in pursuit of perfection and getting down on myself for being that underachieving failure, oblivious to the way others viewed me.

When I started something new, I had to get the best equipment or resources. The problem was that eliminated my excuses, then when I wasn't getting my desired results, I couldn't blame the equipment. I'd have to find something or someone else to blame, or move on so I didn't have to be a failure any longer.

You may have noticed a trend here. First, I was unable to differentiate between failing at something I did and being a failure as a person. Second, I struggled with separating the idea of setting high standards and seeking excellence from setting unrealistic standards and seeking something unachievable. This isn't uncommon among perfectionists as most of us don't know the difference between those two sets of standards. Or more accurately, we know, but aren't able to separate them.

We perfectionists struggle with the simplest of things. A family vacation means a checklist and agenda to see everything in order, on time, and as planned. In my case, with a separate folder for each stop with every reservation, confirmation, site seeing info sheet, etc., all printed out and organized in the most logical sequence. This pattern repeated itself endlessly in my life. Arranging the clothes in the closet, loading the dishwasher, or running errands around town. I was being prepared, planning ahead, getting organized. My family saw an overcontrolling agenda, no flexibility, and a lot less fun.

At some point in my journey, once I admitted my struggle with perfectionism was real, I knew I had to learn more about my addiction. For starters, what exactly is it? Merriam-Webster's dictionary defines perfectionism as a disposition to regard anything short of perfection as unacceptable. Drilling down a little more, perfection is defined as freedom from fault or defect, or an unsurpassable degree of accuracy or excellence. I don't know about you, but when I read that I see error-free excellence jump off the page.

Defining my addiction was only a start. Knowing I needed to get a deeper understanding of what it meant, I did what any good perfectionist would do—research! From the sources available, I relied most heavily on two, *Psychology Today* magazine, and the American Psychological Association website, both of which provided a wealth of original and curated material. So, what do these and other sources they directed me to have to say on the subject?

There are multiple instances where the experts identify two primary types of perfectionism, those being adaptive, and maladaptive. The *Harvard Business Review* refers to these as excellence-seeking perfectionism and failure-avoiding perfectionism, respectively.[1]

Adaptive, or excellence-seeking perfectionism is where the high achievers live. An adaptive perfectionist is someone who sets exceedingly high standards and goals and works very hard to achieve them but recognizes that things may not go perfectly. Generally, an adaptive perfectionist is satisfied with their accomplishments, primarily because they understand the difference between perfection and excellence. Superstar athletes, performers and artists are examples of the types of people grouped into this category.

Take pop superstar Adele as an example. During the 2017 Grammy Awards, Adele performed a tribute to then-recently deceased superstar George Michael. Partway through the song Adele stopped, apologized to the audience, and asked if she could start over because she didn't think her performance was good enough to honor Michael.[2] This wasn't a case of being a failure or not being good enough; it was a case of performance satisfaction for a purpose, perfection required to honor perfection. Another excellence-seeking perfectionist is actress Michelle Pfeiffer, who was once quoted as saying "I'm a perfectionist, so I can drive myself, and other people, mad. At the same time, I think that's one of the reasons I'm successful. Because I really care about what I do. I really want it to be right, and I don't quit until I have to."[3]

Conversely, the maladaptive perfectionist can't differentiate between excellence and perfection. They set high standards and goals, but then beat themselves up with self-criticism and feelings of inadequacy when they don't achieve them. Or, if they do meet their standard, they are mad they didn't perform better or achieve more than they did. Maladaptive perfectionists are never satisfied, usually stressed out, overly critical of themselves and others, and don't hesitate to share the blame for failure. Some research has even indicated that maladaptive perfectionists tend toward depression, obsessive-compulsive disorder, social anxiety, post-traumatic stress disorder, and even suicidal tendencies.[4]

While there isn't a complete consensus on these two classifications, there is general agreement that perfectionism can be broken down into three basic forms identified by Thomas Curran and Andrew Hill in their 2019 paper published in the American Psychological Association Bulletin. These three forms, which they call the multidimensional perfectionism scale, are self-oriented perfectionism, other-oriented perfectionism, and socially-prescribed perfectionism.[5]

Self-oriented perfectionism, like it sounds, is focused on the individual perfectionist and our desire to be perfect. This is the form where we perfectionists set unrealistically high standards for ourselves, think we can't fail because everything depends on us, and believe that being perfect will earn us the credibility and respect we don't think we've earned. Unfortunately, this form of perfectionism is linked to higher levels of depression and anxiety and can contribute to a variety of eating disorders.

Other-oriented perfectionism is when the perfectionist imposes their standards on others, expecting them to achieve the same unreasonable standards the perfectionist sets for themselves. While it may seem the others would be the ones feeling anxious, the perfectionist experiences anxiety as well, worrying about how the others will perform, and if that performance will meet expectations. Perfectionists may also find it challenging to form meaningful relationships and friendships with other people due to imposing unreasonable standards.

Socially-prescribed perfectionism is somewhat of a blend, in that it is essentially other-oriented perfectionism in reverse. In this case, the perfectionist believes others expect them to be perfect, and will only like and respect them if they are. Often, we perfectionists don't think we can live up to the standard set because our feelings of inadequacy tell us we aren't good enough.

These experts and resources have provided me with invaluable insights into myself and my behaviors. Interestingly I find all three forms of perfectionism in myself, at different degrees of affliction, but in all three nonetheless. On a more revealing note, at least to me, I laid out the basic chapters of this book and their intent before I finished all my research. Only as I began writing in earnest did I realize I had organized the first three chapters about the making of the addict in exact alignment with the three forms of perfectionism they described.

While an understanding of the clinical, scientific, or expert information about perfectionism has value, this book is based on my personal experience and observations (and of course research as any good perfectionist would mandate), and delivered from a non-clinical perspective. I'm not a therapist, a counselor, a psychologist, or an addiction specialist. I'm just a regular guy trying to understand himself so he can make his way in the world, perhaps like you.

PERFECTIONISM IS A POWERFUL DRUG, AND ONCE IT GETS A GRIP ON YOU, IT CAN BE DIFFICULT TO BREAK FREE.

Along the way I've come to understand no matter who or what drives us to perfectionism, the earlier we begin the pursuit and the harder we pursue it, the stronger our addiction becomes. Perfectionism is a powerful drug, and once it gets a grip on you, it can be difficult to break free. We strive for perfection until reality sets in, the paradox is revealed, and we expose the damage the pursuit of perfection delivers into our lives. Only then can we break the grip, or at least loosen it so we can move on and reclaim the lives we deserve.

I am grateful you decided to join me on this journey through three stages of perfectionism; ways we develop our addiction to perfection, reflecting on how perfectionism affects our lives, and finally, understanding a path to "recovery" from perfectionism. It's my hope that if you see some of yourself in me, you will overcome your addiction before it breaks you. It took writing this book for me to do it.

PART 1

PERFECTION—THE MAKING OF THE ADDICT

1

I KNOW I CAN DO BETTER

I always feel that whatever I do, I could do better.
I suppose it is perfectionism.

— Rowan Atkinson

Self-imposed perfectionistic tendencies come from a burning internal desire to excel at what we do. The experts call this self-oriented perfection, but I saw it as wanting to do my best. I had one problem, though—it never was. No matter how well I did, I always thought I could have done better. I was never good enough for me.

The earliest memories I have of this feeling of inadequacy go back to little league baseball. I don't remember the exact year, but it was the first season I played in the *majors*, which meant moving up from the small field to the full-size baseball diamond. I made some all-star teams in the *minors* because of my consistently good results, so many in the league had fairly high expectations for my move up.

I set the stage with my first at-bat in the first game of the season. Yep, jacked that pellet out of the park over the right-center field fence. I took my victory trot around the bases, racked up a slew of high fives as I crossed home plate, and, along with my teammates, visualized the huge year I was going to have. Looking back, I have no idea if I had a huge year or not.

I can't remember if I even made the all-star team. In fact, the entire season is lost to me except for two things: that first at-bat home run, and the fact that it was the only one I hit during the entire season. Nothing else mattered at that point because my failure to hit any more home runs defined the whole season as a failure, which of course meant I was a failure. Sure, I played ball for several more years—little league, winter league, high school JV—but it ended there. My childhood dream of playing in the big leagues was dead, mostly because I didn't believe I was good enough anymore after that *horrible* season.

I didn't realize it at the time, but this would be the start of a lifetime struggle with feelings of inadequacy. My experience in scouting is another example. I was active in scouting throughout my youth and worked hard to earn the highest rank at each level: Bear Cub in Cub Scouts; Arrow of Light in Webelos (our den was the first one in the history of the Catalina Council to have every boy in the den earn the Arrow of Light); and finally, Eagle Scout in Boy Scouts. Perfection achieved, right?

I thought so then, but as time progressed, I viewed my accomplishment differently. Scouts were earning their Eagle rank more quickly than I had. I persevered long after many of my friends had given up, receiving my Eagle at nearly seventeen years old, but I read in the quarterly newsletter from the National Eagle Scout Association about scouts as young as 13 achieving Eagle.

My collection of merit badges was a source of pride; I earned 23 of them, more than the 21 required for the rank. That is until reading about a younger scout who had earned all 135 merit badges in existence at that time. Suddenly, my

23 was woefully inadequate. Making matters worse, I never earned a Palm, which is recognition for staying active and earning merit badges after earning Eagle Scout. My failure to earn any Palms became another source of disappointment, especially when considering the young scout who earned all the merit badges also qualified for the maximum number of Palms possible.

Here's the scoop on the negative situation I had manifested. The average age scouts reached Eagle over the last decade was steady at 17 years and three to four months old. As of early 2019, 420 scouts in history have earned every merit badge available. That's less than 0.0004% of all scouts. Finally, less than 1% of Scouts ever earn a Palm.[6] Eagle Scout is an amazing accomplishment, but I came to believe I wasn't a good enough Eagle Scout. Only in my mind could the need to be perfect tarnish such a wonderful accomplishment.

Remember my baseball experience? I didn't mention the reason it ended with the JV team in high school. I got cut from the varsity team at tryouts my junior year. I had a pretty mediocre tryout, so I probably deserved to be cut. I recall hitting two home runs, both off the coach, then him telling me the reason he was cutting me was that I couldn't hit. Kind of ironic, but true. I went out for the track team after that. To clarify, I was 5'-10" tall, a solid 225 lbs., and not so fast. But I was strong, and they had events where all you had to do was throw stuff far. Best of all, track was a no-cut sport!

I picked up the shot put and discus quickly, with discus becoming my favorite. With hard work, I improved and won a few meets. My senior year the chase was on for the school record, and by the end of the season, I threw my personal lifetime best, broke the school record, and qualified for the state championship meet. This may sound exciting, but I'm guessing you know where it's going. I threw the best I could at the state meet but fell short of qualifying for the finals. It didn't matter that I had broken the school record and qualified for the state championships after two seasons in the sport. What did matter was that it was one more thing at which I wasn't good enough.

For perfectionists, our thinking fuels our need for perfection, and we intentionally place ourselves into the *perfect* spiral. When we fail, we become depressed, angry, and embarrassed. Because we must not fail, we strive harder for perfection, making us more depressed, angry, and embarrassed when we *do* fail. So, what do we do? We ratchet up the effort level even more, and well, you get the picture.

> FOR PERFECTIONISTS, OUR THINKING FUELS OUR NEED FOR PERFECTION, AND WE INTENTIONALLY PLACE OURSELVES INTO THE *PERFECT* SPIRAL.

Surely this can't be our fault, can it? We tried so hard and did so well; there must be someone or something else to blame. Nope.

The perfectionist just sees themselves as inadequate. Julia Cameron, an artist and author of *The Artists Way, The Prosperous Heart: Creating a Life of "Enough"*, and over 30 other books, captured it this way: "Perfectionism is not a quest for the best. It is a pursuit of the worst in ourselves, the part that tells us that nothing we do will ever be good enough—that we should try again."

That's a big problem. We've spiraled ourselves into a point of not being able to tell the difference between failing and being a failure. To make up for our shortcomings, we often have to prove our worth in other ways. Brené Brown is a University of Houston professor, TEDx speaker, and author of *The Gifts of Imperfection,* as well as several other books on perfection, shame, and vulnerability. She contends perfection is not about healthy achievement, growth, or self-improvement, but is about it being a shield, and a tool for gaining the approval and acceptance of others.

I can vouch for Brené's thoughts from my personal experience. My feelings of inadequacy didn't end with scouting and high school sports; they followed me into adulthood and my career. I won't bore you with every step of my career, but there are highlights demonstrating my continuing spiral into inadequacy and failure.

In nearly 35 years of experience, I'm on my 11th employer. A few stops lasted six to seven years each so you can do the math on the rest. Some people might call that job-hopping, but I called it climbing the career ladder. After leaving my first employer, I worked for four different consulting engineering firms in seven years. Along the way, I had a five-month stop at one, but believed my departure from that job was not my fault, and I worked hard to prove that.

Two other firms went out of business shortly after my 15- to 18-month tenures with them ended. When offered the job at the fourth consulting firm, I asked if they were sure they wanted to hire me because I had put two of the previous firms out of business. It was offered as humor, but you and I both know there was some serious thought behind it of *did I really have anything to do with those firms going out of business?*

At age 40, I became Director of Transportation for the 38th largest city in the country at the time, earning a comfortable six figures. It was a job I earned and loved, but after a few years, I made the move to a similar opportunity in a neighboring city, where I happened to live. I decided the new position would be more challenging and prestigious because an airport was added to my responsibilities, and it allowed me to serve my community.

My tenure there lasted just over four months, with my dismissal coming the week between Christmas and New Year's. It was unexpected, and I was furious because I felt it was completely unwarranted. Fortunately, I landed in a great place with a successful consulting firm, but that contract came to an end nearly seven years later, launching another cycle through a revolving door of three different employers in five years. The first two of those ended when conditions or superiors changed, so those really couldn't be my fault either. Do you see the pattern? I couldn't stay in a stable situation too long for fear of eventually being found out, so I regularly moved into positions that didn't work out. Of course, when they didn't work out, it wasn't my fault, right?

I thought I wasn't a good enough employee, an imposter in their midst, so I made up for it by collecting credentials and recognition. I became a registered professional engineer in three states, won several project and personal awards, and was elected national president of a professional association full of high-caliber people. My favorite accomplishment was my collection of numerous professional certifications and designations. I was proud of what I had become—Jeffrey A. Kramer, PE, PWLF, CPM, CCM, TCS, CJP, CHBC. Maybe now I was finally good enough.

In reviewing that signature line, my name has 14 letters in it, but my credentials have 22 letters in them—more letters in my credentials than in my name. There were so many I had to drop some to get down to 12 credential letters so they fit on my business card. I was proud of the collection and thought if I had all those certifications from credential-issuing organizations, people would respect me, and I would appear good enough. But it had little impact. I merely felt more inadequate because now I had all these credentials to live up to, yet knew I probably wouldn't.

What does my ancient history have to do with anything? It's the foundation of my addiction. Throughout my life, I chased perfection because I never thought I was good enough. I knew I could do better and was addicted to achieving the ideal. For many perfectionists, this is the way we're built. This internal wiring, or behavioral tendency if you will, often draws perfectionist-oriented people into career fields where mistakes are costly, so being perfect is seen as an asset. Think engineers, architects, accountants, surgeons, and so on. If you are familiar with the DISC model of human behavior, we are the Cs.

DISC is a behavior model developed in the 1920s by Dr William Moulton Marston, who later went on to contribute to the invention of the lie detector, and also to create the character Wonder Woman. The DISC model predicts a person's normal behavior tendencies based on two traits; the speed at which they engage with others, and whether they tend to focus on productivity or relationships. Depending on the blend of traits, Marston described the styles as Dominant and Driving (D), Inspiring and Interactive (I), Supportive and Steady (S), or Cautious and Competent (C).

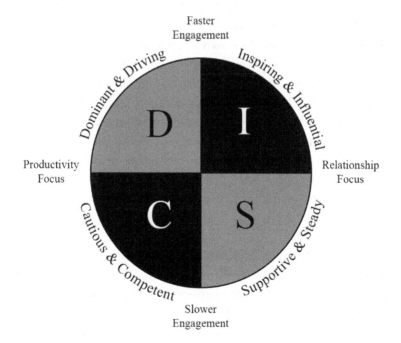

Since many perfectionists fall into the C behavioral style, let's focus on that briefly. Approximately 25% of the population falls into the type C personality category. This personality type is generally slower to engage with others and tends to think instead of feel. We like consistency, quality and excellence, doing things properly, and we value logic, credibility, intellect, stability, and understanding why. We also tend to be pessimistic (although we see it as being realistic), overly organized, and overly analytical. [7] If you've ever heard the phrase *analysis paralysis*, that's a C type personality.

Being a C isn't a bad place to be. Famous people who share this perfectionist tendency include Bill Gates, Albert Einstein, and Steve Jobs (during his first stint at Apple). Michael Jackson, the musical genius behind *Thriller, Billie Jean, Beat It,* and dozens of other chart-topping hits, is another good example of a C type personality. During a 1993 interview with Oprah Winfrey, Jackson said, "I'm never pleased with anything, I'm a perfectionist, it's part of who I am."

He even admitted to crying after doing the moonwalk for the first time on the Motown 25th anniversary special, not because he was happy with performing a move no one had ever done before, but because he was unhappy with how it had gone.[8] Imagine, the person many consider the greatest entertainer of his time pulls off a new, now-iconic dance move, and he wasn't satisfied. Music producer Akon later noted that if he hadn't pushed Jackson to release his music, he might never have put out a song.[9] Numerous experts suspect Jackson's ultra-perfectionism contributed to the sleep deprivation and depression issues that ultimately led to his 2009 death from heart failure caused by a medication overdose.

Winston Churchill nailed it for this personality type when he stated, "The maxim 'nothing but perfection' may be spelled 'paralysis.'"[10] Paralysis is the perfect description, pun intended. Churchill probably should have said we are paralyzed by fear. The fear of failing and therefore, being viewed less favorably in some way, and the fear of being embarrassed or being found out to be an imposter are common.

My biggest fear is whatever I do or create will not be good enough, meaning I am not good enough, thus making me a complete failure, again. I can't count the number of things that sit unfinished or never got started, because of this paralysis. Someone only needs to look around my yard, garage, house, office, or even on my hard drive for proof. Dozens of ideas and plans were laid to rest by fear of failure over not being good enough. Writing this book may be one of the biggest. Actually, it didn't start out as this book.

In late September 2013, I was attending the 25th American Academy of Certified Public Managers® conference in Boise, Idaho. While there, my wife, Sharon, and I went out to dinner with my boss. Joining us were my friend, Phillip, and his wife, Susan. Phil, who was keynoting the conference, is an accomplished executive, a highly sought-after speaker, and an author with several books to his credit.

During conversation, I announced I was writing a book and asked Phil if he would read it and consider writing the foreword or an endorsement. At the time, I was planning a personal growth book, roughly titled *The Keys to Unlocking Your Peak Performance*. I created a directory folder and document file for it on my computer, but that's as far as it got. I never started writing because I was afraid no one would want to read it. After all, what had I ever done?

Eventually, the idea morphed into a leadership book, which included the same beginning and ending as the other concept. I had been presenting on the topic for that book, and had ideas for a coaching program as well. I even recorded 14 videos and created handouts for the program. But I was afraid it wouldn't be good enough, so neither the book nor the program has seen the light of day. The leadership book was important to me, though, so I needed to conquer my fear.

This is around the time my perfection addiction was exposed, and I began working toward overcoming it. Facing my perfectionism head-on was the only way I could move forward with everything I wanted to accomplish, including the leadership book and program. That's when I realized I had to write this book before I could be free to do anything else. I committed to contributing the finances, and to a completion deadline, but, even then, the introduction and this first chapter took me five months to write and submit to editorial review. I was so afraid it would suck that I was paralyzed and couldn't get started.

For me, it's been a lifetime of paralysis from the fear I wouldn't be good enough. Can you relate? Thinking you can do better no matter what it is or how well you've done is debilitating. You've had a glimpse of how much life I've lost by standing still because I was afraid to step forward. How much life have you lost to thinking you weren't good enough and could do better?

Before you move on to the next chapter, stop and think seriously about that question. Grab a piece of paper and jot down all the times you didn't do something because you were afraid you weren't good enough. Then list everything you did to hide those imperfections. How does your list look? Reflect on how the items you listed have held you back. It's a bit of an *ouch* moment, isn't it?

If only we had gotten some help or encouragement along the way from parents, teachers, a coach, or a boss.

2

YOUR LETTERING IS OFF

Perfectionism rarely begets perfection, or satisfaction—
only disappointment.

— Ryan Holiday

L iving up to the expectations of others is challenging in general, but when those others are people we love, trust, and respect, those challenges take on new meaning. No one wants to let their parents down, so when Mom and Dad encourage us to do better next time, we try to make our next effort perfect. The same thing happens when Coach says we need to improve our technique, or Teacher tells us our work isn't quite right. We need to make the starting line-up, get straight A's, or get that promotion, and the way we think we can get there is by being perfect. At least I did.

In school, I was an honor student and overachiever. I recall studying for an exam one night in high school. I don't remember what the subject was anymore, but I asked my mom to quiz me. At one point, she thought I gave a wrong answer, but I told her I knew my answer was right, what page it was on, and where on that page the answer could be found. I don't have a photographic memory; I was so intent on getting the best grade possible that I had memorized everything about what I was studying.

It wasn't only the "rigorous" classes that caused this behavior. In my high school architectural drafting class, we had an assignment to work on our lettering by printing the alphabet. It wasn't just any old printing though.

Try to recall when you were first learning to write; your paper probably had sets of parallel horizontal lines defining the bottom and the top of your letters. In drafting class, we had an extra line to define the top of our upper- and lower-case letters separately. Our lettering had to be vertical and within those lines. If the letters weren't vertical enough, or were too short or tall, we had to redo the alphabet until they were perfect.

I have no idea how many tries it took me, but I'm pretty sure I eventually got it right since I passed the class. If you've ever heard stories from people who attended Catholic school about nuns smacking them across the knuckles if their handwriting wasn't good enough, then you'll understand how I felt.

Have you ever tried to satisfy someone with your work but felt you couldn't quite get there? Most people try to do a little better, get the work done, and move on. For perfectionists, it becomes another frustrating, demoralizing experience in validating our inadequacy. To compensate, we try harder and harder until we get it right. My printing? Well into my adult life, I still held to the practice of starting over and rewriting notes if my printing got the slightest bit sloppy.

What I remember most from that architectural drafting class is having a great teacher who also happened to be my track and field coach. He always wanted the best for me, my classmates, and my teammates. Coach Mayfield often allowed me the freedom to explore ideas and do special assignments for him. He encouraged me to do my best, but when things didn't go my way, he also encouraged me to figure out how I could improve from what I had learned or experienced.

Coach Mayfield never told me I had to be perfect, never said I couldn't compete in the next meet if my technique wasn't right or if I didn't get better every week. He encouraged me to improve my form and pushed me to perform better every meet, but there was no punishment from him if I didn't. That all came from me. I'd win a meet, but would be disappointed if I didn't achieve a new personal best, then I'd be grumpy and solemn all night. My folks must have thought I was mental, and in a way, they would have been right.

These high school memories probably sound more like a yearbook than a book about perfectionism, but let me share one more before I move on to the point.

I was crazy about photography back then. We had an incredible group of student photographers on the photojournalism staff who took most of the newspaper and yearbook photos. One of my former classmates is now a professional photographer. Our teacher/advisor, Phil Burton, who has sadly passed on, was supportive but demanding.

Mr Burton never told me my composition had to be exquisite, my exposure exact, or my focus flawless. I'm not Ansel Adams after all. He expected me to do quality work that was good enough to print in a high school newspaper or yearbook. And he wanted to see improvement with each assignment.

How did this translate in my mind? Like any normal person, I took all the clothes out of my closet at home and converted it into a darkroom so I could practice and improve when the school darkroom was closed. I even convinced my dad to plumb running water through the wall of the house into the closet so I could have a live rinse tray. Normal person, right? But my photography needed to be perfect!

Most people would be thrilled to have had the amazing support I received. I was, and still am, grateful for all of it. But I managed to turn it into something else, something punishing. How could I have academic successes like being inducted into the National Honor Society and graduating in the top 10% of my class, but focus on things like not having earned a perfect 4.0 average or being awarded the scholarships I needed to attend my first-choice university? Or second. Or third. My answer—I wasn't good enough.

> SOMEHOW, I MANAGED TO TRANSLATE DO *YOUR* BEST TO DO *THE* BEST, THOUGH, AND I COULDN'T MEET THAT STANDARD FOR MYSELF.

The irony is that my folks never pushed me to be perfect; they wanted me to do my best, just like Coach Mayfield, Mr Burton, and all my coaches and teachers up to that stage of life. Do the best I was capable of, and they would be happy. That's it. Somehow, I managed to translate do *your* best to do *the* best, though, and I couldn't meet that standard for myself.

While most people look back at high school as the time of their lives and stayed connected with their friends, I didn't miss high school at all, and it took me until a couple of years ago to start reconnecting with many of those old friends.

Thank goodness we get to go to college, start fresh with new friends and teachers, maybe join a fraternity or some clubs. Now that's the life, right? You would think so, but college wasn't a big change for me. As an engineering student, I was a hard worker aiming for perfection, but missing by a wide margin. I was average, roughly a 3.0 student who never quite reached my potential. One professor told me I should be doing so much better, and that perhaps I should take a shot of tequila before exams to help me relax a little. If that was a hint, I missed it.

The pressure of not being good enough caused me to consider dropping out of engineering school to become a history teacher instead. I stayed with it though and did get out with my engineering degree, but I couldn't get the jobs I really wanted. One interviewer even told me point blank, "Why would you think you could ever work for us when you got Bs and Cs in your structural design classes?" Maybe the joke's on him since I did work for that company ten years into my career, but fresh out of school I wasn't good enough.

Employment was simply the next sequence in the crazy pattern where I applied pressure on myself to do better than others expected of me. I did it as a little leaguer, as a high school student-athlete, and as a college student. Then I let those experiences set the stage for my career and life experiences.

I'm sure my job experience isn't all that different than yours. You start at entry-level, work hard, hopefully, get a promotion or two along the way, and eventually, you get to your dream job. I hope that didn't make you choke as it did me. Yes, I started entry-level and worked hard. Yes, I got a promotion or two along the way. But I also made a lot of changes. Remember those 11 employers in 35 years?

Along the way, I had some terrific bosses, and some that had a lot of room for improvement. No matter how good or bad, though, I learned something from each of them. No offense to the many good bosses I've had over the years, but the one who left the lasting impression that shaped me more than any other was Pam Lowe.

Pam was a young female engineer crushing it in the male-dominated world of civil engineering for the state transportation department. She was a brilliant, commanding, beautiful, influential, and somewhat intimidating rising star who had an incredible future ahead. I was an entry-level engineer in my first job out of college, and Pam was assembling a new unit to oversee projects around the state.

I worked for her briefly during one of my training rotations, and was fortunate she selected me for her new team. We worked hard as a unit to earn the respect of our peers inside and outside the agency, but we also had a lot of fun. Once, one of my co-workers and I, both University of Arizona graduates, taped Wildcat rah-rah items all over Pam's window before the big rivalry game with her Arizona State Sun Devils and closed her blinds. Imagine her surprise when she opened them!

What I remember most was how thoroughly Pam prepared us for everything. She had that knack for knowing what to expect, then helped us prepare for it. She would sit with us in her office and quiz us to ensure we were ready for any question or angle. I never went before the project review committee to ask for additional time or money without having every answer. Pam's team members were always the best-prepared people in the room, and I found myself wanting to make her look good the way I knew how—by being perfect.

When I became a supervisor years later, I wanted to have the most prepared team, always ready for anything, so I followed her lead and expected perfection from my people. At least that's how I twisted the lessons she taught me. The great football coach Vince Lombardi once said, "Perfection is not attainable, but if we chase perfection, we can catch excellence." In my pursuit of perfection, I had once again lost sight of excellence, which is what Pam expected of us and taught us to pursue.

Does any of this sound familiar? Have you felt like you couldn't let someone down, so you put so much pressure on yourself that it was almost unbearable? That's what we perfectionists do. There's no middle ground—it's all or nothing.

Perfectionists overuse the words *always* and *never* because we either succeed or fail. We find our identities in approval from those we are trying to please. When this happens, we become our results; they define our self-esteem and self-image. When we succeed, we are winners, especially if told how perfect our effort was. But when we stumble or make a mistake, which happens more often than not for most perfectionists because of our high standards, we are failures. We're embarrassed or ashamed, and feel guilty for letting ourselves or someone else down.

Going from winner to loser is an easy transition for a perfectionist to make. Several years ago, my father asked me to help him with a couple of small projects over the course of a few months. He needed to pave a small parking area in front of his business, and the City of Phoenix was paving the streets in the area, so I drew up a simple plan he used to get the city's contractor to complete the paving for him. The City was happy, so was he, and I was a winner.

A few months later, my father asked me for help again, this time to get measurements for an airplane hangar opening so he could order a custom door. I correctly measured the opening width of 43'-2" but the door that arrived was 42'-3" wide. I'm guessing you know where this is going. I transposed numbers, leaving the door 11 inches shy. My father framed a narrow filler section with windows on one side of the opening, and told me dozens of times how much better it turned out since the filler section gave him the chance to add some natural light into an otherwise dark space. But to me, I was just a failure who screwed up his hangar door.

It's so easy for a perfectionist to turn a resolved mistake into a lasting failure, a valuable lesson into an unachievable goal, or an expectation for excellence into a demand for perfection.

Think about when you took the well-intentioned support of a parent, advice of a boss, or direction from a coach, and warped it into something it was never intended to be, feeding your need to be better than they expected. Did you come up with multiple examples? My guess is you did.

With all this perfection going on in professional environments, it sure would be nice to socialize with friends and family in a way that I didn't have to be so darn perfect, right?

3

OH SNAP, FACEBOOK MADE ME DO IT!

Everyone is comparing lives on social media and wants the perfect body, perfect image, perfect outfit, perfect life—we're striving for this perfection, and it's so unhealthy because there's no such thing as perfection.

— Emily Atack

The pressures we feel to be perfect are often societal. We try to live up to expectations created by people we "know" but who don't directly impact our lives. One cause of this "perfection envy" is the media and its portrayal of celebrities, sports superstars, models, and others in the limelight. An even bigger offender is social media. We spend so much time trying to emulate what we see on social media channels, not realizing we are attempting to match our everyday lives to filtered and edited highlight reels. Radio personality and author Charlamagne tha God, who is well known for calling people out on his program *The Breakfast*

Club, said, "I think social media is painting an unattainable picture of perfection."

There's no shortage of opportunities to see those highlight reels. When I was a kid, social media didn't exist. If you wanted to know what your friends were up to, you either called them or jumped on your bike and rode to their house. Your friends were limited to people in proximity to you unless you met someone from another school or town at camp or on vacation, who you then communicated with through phone calls and letters.

Now we have hundreds or thousands of "friends" from around the world, many we've never met but we "know" someone in common or have a mutual interest or affiliation. By some estimates, there are currently over three billion people on at least one social media platform. And we all friend, follow, like, connect, snap, tweet, view, share and pin everything we do, everywhere we go, and more. We are connected in ways I never imagined as a kid, and that's as bad as it is good.

In the Curran and Hill paper mentioned in the introduction, the authors identified the three basic forms of perfectionism as self-oriented perfectionism, other-oriented perfectionism, and socially prescribed perfectionism. This paper reviewed nearly 60 research studies conducted around the world between 1989 and 2016, and performed additional independent research.

As I said before, I'm not a psychologist or therapist, and admittedly there were aspects of their work that were a bit too technical in the psychology field for me. One point was made clear—the form of perfectionism that saw the largest increase during the study was socially prescribed perfectionism, which many experts most closely link to eating disorders and mental illnesses.

Multiple studies have shown a correlation between social media's influence on comparison and perfectionism with negative impacts to people's health by increasing feelings of depression and inadequacy, especially in teenagers and millennials. The Curran and Hill research showed college students averaged over an hour per day on social media, mostly creating a public image that suggested perfection in their lives, no matter how inaccurate. Curran and Hill went on to say "exposure to others' perfect self-representations within social media can intensify one's own body image concerns and sense of social alienation."[5]

Although I've lived the perfection spiral mentioned in chapter one multiple times, I didn't realize it or understand it. However, Canadian psychologist Paul Hewitt does. In his book *Perfectionism: A Relational Approach to Conceptualization, Assessment, and Treatment* he stated that "perfectionism isn't about perfecting things: your job, a specific project, the way you look, or a relationship. At a fundamental level, it's about perfecting the self, and this urge doesn't come from a healthy place. All components and dimensions of perfectionism ultimately involve attempts to perfect an imperfect self."

Hewitt and his co-authors went on to indicate that perfectionist traits start at a young age with the assumption "If I'm perfect, I won't be rejected, ridiculed, abused, I'll be loved and accepted. It's an unconscious negotiation they make with the world: If I'm perfect, all this good stuff will happen, all these needs will be met, and their frequently difficult relationships with parents, siblings, and peers will become easier."[11]

There it is. Perfection is all about acceptance and being good enough for others. As humans, we're biologically, physically and spiritually wired to love and be loved, and to belong to a group.

Maslow's Hierarchy of Needs, a model of human motivational theory developed by psychologist Abraham Maslow in the 1940s, is based on the assumption that people must meet basic needs before progressing to social, or psychological needs. These must then be met before achieving full potential as individuals. The model is often shown as a triangle, with basic needs at the bottom, and mastery and fulfillment at the top.

Maslow's Heirarchy of Needs

What Hewitt describes, then, falls directly into the love and belonging level, intimating that perfectionists may find ourselves stuck and never able to achieve self-esteem or fulfillment if we don't obtain social acceptance. This further drives our pursuit of perfection, and when we don't fulfill those needs for acceptance and approval, we fall apart, get sick, become depressed, or worse. Through social media, we can seek the approval of others, fulfilling our social needs from people we may not even know or ever meet.

My friend, Renee Vidor, who identifies herself as a "comparaholic," explains how comparing yourself to others is a recipe for unhappiness in her book *Measuring Up: How to Win In A World Of Comparison*. While her book isn't about perfectionism specifically, I recently heard Renee speak, and the parallels are amazing. In her presentation, Renee stated that "We steer where we stare," which essentially means we are going to move in the direction of our focus. She then went on to outline three roadblocks that comparison causes, those being assets, appearances, and achievements. She is absolutely right. We tend to focus on other's assets, appearances, and achievements, then compare our lives to theirs.

Let's consider this from a perfectionist's perspective. When I looked at my social media feeds, I saw "friends" on vacations in exotic faraway places, buying fancy new cars or homes, getting promotions or new jobs, signing big contracts, and landing new clients. It was overflowing with things, places and accomplishments I didn't have or couldn't see happening for myself. Did you catch that? Things, places, and accomplishments, much like assets, appearances, and achievements. Do your social media feeds make you feel the same way?

Famous feminist, journalist, and Presidential Medal of Freedom recipient, Gloria Steinem once said, "Perfectionism attaches to what is valued in the culture." While a comparaholic might try to keep pace with what they see in their social media feeds, I would tell myself I was a failure because someone else (society/culture) had or did something (assets/appearances/achievements) I thought was out of reach. I became anxious, and the competitive streak kicked in. I had to post about what I had, what I did, where I went and more, not in a bid to be connected, but to relieve my anxiety about being a failure by showing everyone that I really was good enough. Thanks a lot, Facebook!

In reality, it wasn't my "friends" or contacts making me feel inferior. That was all my doing. Like I did with my internal drive, and with encouragement I received from others, I took my social media feeds to new heights of reinterpretation. If my life couldn't look like what I saw in my feed then why even try—it would never measure up? What should have been happiness for others, or something taken with the proverbial "grain of salt," became food for my feelings of inadequacy.

Now think about the fantastic social media feeds we see from celebrities and influencers. They have the perfect life, the perfect physique, the perfect companion. Whatever they posted was perfect, and we wanted it. Intuitively we know they have a team of people doing their makeup and hair, fitting their wardrobe, photoshopping the images to remove blemishes and be amazing, and more. It's not real, but we still see it and think, "I want that."

Influencers and thought-leaders are continuously adding top quality content to keep their following engaged, and we regular folk have to add more and better content if we want to reach influencer or thought-leader status. In some cases that status is tied to significant income through sponsors, product placement, or advertising, further driving the need to have that perfect feed. Actress Lana Condor captured this when she said "We are so sucked into our screens, and our life is so curated. You see other perfect lives and your life isn't like that, so if I go out and people see that my life isn't perfect, I'm afraid they'll judge me."

Unfortunately, social media platforms are built around creating comparison and envy, providing a way to self-promote like a peacock on display for a potential mate. As soon as you create your profile, you are asked questions to categorize you, helping to customize the algorithm for what you see and how you're seen. Fortunately, some platforms are paying attention. Snapchat and TikTok, arguably the two hottest platforms of today, don't have feedback features like comments and "likes," and in mid-2019, Instagram tested doing away with "likes" for some U.S. users.

> UNFORTUNATELY, SOCIAL MEDIA PLATFORMS ARE BUILT AROUND CREATING COMPARISON AND ENVY, PROVIDING A WAY TO SELF-PROMOTE LIKE A PEACOCK ON DISPLAY FOR A POTENTIAL MATE.

Have you ever experienced this social media envy, or worse, social media inadequacy? Think about when you have, and what caused you to feel that way. Did it genuinely affect your life, or did you allow it to? I understand because that's what I did.

Whether your pursuit of perfection was self-inflicted, prompted by a reinterpretation of input from others, societally driven, or, as in my case, a thorough combination of all three, we drank the Kool-Aid and became perfectionists. If the making of a perfectionist wasn't enough, we then have to experience life inside the paradox our perfectionism creates for us.

PART 2

PARALYSIS—
LIFE INSIDE THE
PARADOX

4

I'LL GET TO IT TOMORROW, OR THE NEXT DAY, OR MAYBE FRIDAY . . .

Perfectionism is a distraction, a justification for
procrastination, an excuse for never getting anything done.
It is a refusal to accept reality, and it is rooted in fear.
To the perfectionist, nothing will ever be good enough.

— Dr Henry Cloud

One of the most common effects of perfection on our lives is the tendency to procrastinate. Or, as Napoleon Hill defines it, "Procrastination is the bad habit of putting off until the day after tomorrow, what should have been done the day before yesterday." In my opinion, procrastination is probably the most damaging aspect of perfectionism. It is detrimental enough on its own, but worse than that, it's the starting point for a multitude of deeper behavioral and emotional issues.

For some people, procrastination is a choice, a conscious decision to avoid doing something undesirable or challenging.

Students are a great example of this. I have four daughters who recently were or still are in college, and I see them doing the same things I did when I was a student. Don't want to do that homework assignment? No problem, just put it off until right before it's due, then pull an all-nighter. Exam coming up soon? There's plenty of time to cram in that last 24-hours.

For a perfectionist, procrastination may be a choice, or it may be more about anxiety, self-doubt and fear. When all those things combine, fear of failure includes anxiety over what will happen if you fail, and fear you can't meet your own expectations or do the job right. Not *won't*, but *can't*. It's an involuntary behavioral tendency, the type that affects us even with things important to us. Goals, dreams and aspirations get pushed to the wayside because we are afraid we won't achieve them, or if we do, we will be disappointed in the results.

It isn't only the delay that gets us. After putting things off for too long, we try to restart, hoping to improve upon what we originally put off. When we don't think we can, we stop and delay again, then start the cycle all over. We restart until we are blue in the face, then conclude it isn't good enough to finish. So we quit or file it away under the heading of "things I'll get back to someday."

Unfortunately, someday doesn't exist on any calendar, so it never comes, and neither does the opportunity we missed as a result. Even though many people will see an opportunity right in front of them, a perfectionist will continue to wait until the last minute, doing nothing until we know everything's right. The bad news is no one is ever guaranteed a second chance at an opportunity, especially a missed one.

Jen Sincero, author of *You Are A Badass, How to Stop Doubting Your Greatness and Start Living an Awesome Life,* said, "Perfectionism and procrastination have such a fine line. You say, 'Well, I want it to be good. I want it to be perfect.' But what you're really doing is not doing your work. You're putting off showing up and being visible because then you're going to be judged, and it might suck."

Jen hits the nail on the head with this one. Procrastination is not the problem; it's the judgement and fear. Yep, it's that simple. We put things off because we are afraid. Afraid that no one will like it; that it will have a mistake, which is, of course, unacceptable; that we will be ridiculed or embarrassed; that it will be judged harshly; or the ultimate fear, that it will prove what we already believe to be true, that we aren't good enough.

In his book *The War of Art*, Steven Pressfield calls this "The Resistance." He describes this as an ever-present force working to prevent us from accomplishing whatever we are attempting. If you are a person of faith, as I am, you call this The Enemy. Pressfield says, "Resistance is the most toxic force on the planet. It arises from within and takes the shape of procrastination, lack of motivation, insecurities, self-doubt, fear and what not." He goes on to say "Procrastination is the most common manifestation of resistance because it's the easiest to rationalize. We don't tell ourselves 'I'm never going to write that book.' Instead, we say, 'I'm going to do it tomorrow,' but tomorrow never comes."[12] There's that *someday* rearing its ugly head again.

I experienced all of that with this book. I jumped right into the development process when I signed with my publisher, then stopped when I had to write a chapter. After a few months passed, I forced myself to push through the fear and get it written. It was excruciating. I cried when I submitted it to my publisher for editorial review. And then another pause. I spent the next few months convinced this was all a mistake and I didn't have it in me to write a book. Finally, I was challenged by one of my coaches to get just three chapters written and sent to her within 45 days, so I did. I cranked out Chapters 1-3 in Part 1 without too much self-editing, and better yet, without fear of whether it was good or not. It was simply done.

Taking action is critical when it comes to living in the paradox, especially regarding procrastination. While striving for perfection may sound good, the reality is that imperfect action beats perfect inaction every time. Not some of the time. Every. Single. Time.

> WHILE STRIVING FOR PERFECTION MAY SOUND GOOD, THE REALITY IS THAT IMPERFECT ACTION BEATS PERFECT INACTION EVERY TIME.

Unfortunately, it's not that simple. Perfectionists are so afraid of not being perfect that we paralyze ourselves with fear, with obsessing over details, overthinking the what-ifs, or with anything else that might need our extended attention or consideration. To break free of the analysis paralysis, we rationalize our procrastination. It becomes easy to say things like "I wouldn't have done it right anyway, so probably just as well I didn't waste time on it," or "I don't know enough to create that product/program, so I'll do something else instead." Do those sound familiar?

As an engineer, I know how to analyze things; it's in my DNA. But when is the analysis enough? One of the ways procrastination manifested inside the paradox for me was through analysis paralysis, or never-ending data collection and analysis. I collected, studied, and learned well past the point of value, but I *needed* all of that information to know enough, have enough, and get good enough. I never believed I was getting there, though, so the rationalization began.

I told myself I needed to learn more before I would know enough to coach someone else. That I couldn't write a book because I didn't know enough about perfection. Ironic, isn't it? I let my perfectionism drive me to procrastinate about writing a book on perfectionism. Analysis paralysis is a common procrastination tactic, because it allows those of us inclined to that type of behavior to have an easy excuse, and don't we all love easy!

Another way procrastination shows up is through the need for the perfect time, place or conditions to exist before taking action. Ever say to yourself "I will ask for a raise when the time is right," or "I need to be in the right frame of mind to take that on." For a perfectionist, we need everything to be just right before we can start. If condition one exists, then we also want to make sure conditions two and three are going to happen before some specific time or deadline we've set, usually arbitrarily and unrealistically. Crazy, I know, but if it doesn't all fall into place, then a perfectionist won't even make the attempt. It won't be the right time, the right place, under the right set of conditions, with the right person, and so on.

Imagine you are proposing to your longtime partner. You've planned the perfect night, with a gourmet dinner, romantic music, and the first-class venue is in on it. Everything is just right, perfect actually. Right before you pop the question, something goes wrong. A plate smashes in the background, or an ambulance screams by outside. Seemingly insignificant to some people, but how would it affect you? For some, it would bring the night to its knees, killing the mood, and perhaps delaying the ask.

What about completing a special project assigned to you, perhaps one you actively pursued? If you're like me, you spend time organizing the project by thinking about the process and desired results, defining the goals, and developing a step-by-step action plan. I always thought of it as a construction project in need of a detailed work breakdown structure with time and resource allocation.

Then you start thinking about what might go wrong, you know, performing the risk analysis. Now we have to develop a contingency plan for each of those things that might go wrong, so we aren't caught unprepared if they do. Then the worry starts. What if all those things go wrong? It would derail the project, and that would be a big blow. Hmmm, maybe I'd be better off not going down that path at all. In fact, perhaps I should put this off for a while and think about it some more. And there you have it. I've analyzed myself right into the perfect procrastination spiral again.

It's happened to me over and over. Writing a book, creating an online course, launching a podcast, developing a live conference event—all things I was excited about doing, but self-sabotaged in one way or another. That's a key to living inside the paradox. Eventually you might get around to doing whatever you put off, so all you've done is fooled yourself into losing time, and potentially income, influence, impact, and legacy. Ouch.

That's a painful realization, but it comes late in the process. Each time I put off one of my projects, I didn't feel pain, only relief. Why? I delayed pursuing a goal or dream I wanted to accomplish because I was afraid things might go wrong before I ever gave it a chance. That's what perfectionism does to us.

The feeling of relief we get from procrastinating is perfectionism masked as a rush of endorphins coming to reduce our stress and anxiety. Unfortunately, it works more like a drug than an endorphin, turning procrastination into a perfectionist's natural Xanax. When we come down from the initial high, that relief turns into self-inflicted pain, and those feelings of inadequacy and failure come rushing back. Hockey great Wayne Gretzky once said, "Procrastination is one of the most common and deadliest of diseases and its toll on success and happiness is heavy."

Let's look at the flip side, a time when not procrastinating made a difference. On September 11, 2001, the world was rocked by the hijacking of several passenger airline flights in the United States. If you were old enough at the time, I have no doubt you remember exactly where you were and what you were doing that morning when the news broke that a plane had flown into the World Trade Center in New York City, killing hundreds.

Then, a second plane struck.

While the world watched in horror, a third plane flew into the Pentagon.

What does any of this have to do with procrastination? There was a fourth plane that morning, United Flight 93. The passengers aboard that flight discovered what was happening and decided to take action. Then came those famous words, passenger Todd Beamer saying, "Let's Roll."

Beamer and his fellow passengers attacked the hijackers, causing the plane to crash into an open field in Pennsylvania. While 44 people died in that crash, the action those passengers took saved an unknown number of lives that may never be countable. Was the target the White House, the Capitol, a nuclear plant? Thankfully, we will never know because Beamer and others, at the cost of their own lives, did not procrastinate. [13]

Putting things off may not be a life or death situation for you—it hasn't been for me—but it certainly was life-damaging. The feelings of overwhelm, inadequacy, and dread caused me to put off important things for less important ones. I fell short of goals, letting myself and others down. I even put off getting healthy because I convinced myself I couldn't lose weight without exercising, but couldn't exercise because being overweight made it too painful. Then I would beat myself up mentally for putting off what I knew I should do. I was successfully creating a life of missed opportunities and failures that plagued me for years.

5

THAT SHOULD DO IT, OR THAT, OR THAT . . .

The pursuit of perfection often impedes improvement.

— George Will

While I've sampled the many ways perfection manifests itself, the continuous pursuit of "better" affected me the most. This is the perfectionistic area I still struggle with more than any other. Addiction to the ideal drives an incessant need to revise, tweak, review, start over and more. The product or result never meets the impossible standard set, so we must improve on it indefinitely. But, no matter how many times we try, the result is never good enough. That's how perfectionists are. We aren't as much concerned about being perfect as we are about not being good enough, which continually puts our focus on failure rather than success.

The worst part is we never know when it's time to stop revising and let it be good enough—time to let the task, product or project come to an end. For a non-perfectionist, everything eventually has a conclusion, but for the perfection-ist, everything has a point of failure or giving up.

Artist Alexander Calder said, "To an engineer, good enough means perfect. With an artist, there's no such thing as perfect." Calder and I never met, but I feel as though he knew me. I could take something as simple as writing a note and turn it into an exercise in frustration. As soon as my lettering looked less than perfect to me, I would toss that version in the trash and start over.

Imagine taking notes in a lecture, workshop, or at a conference. If you've done so, you know it can be challenging to keep up with the presenter, so abbreviations and symbols are helpful. Once home, I would rewrite all my notes, not because I wanted to absorb the learning or fix the material in my mind, but because they were far too sloppy for me. Of course, the rewrite usually took multiple attempts.

When I say multiple, I'm not kidding. At times, I wouldn't even get past the first line, and the page would be in a ball in the trash. I even put one of those mini basketball hoops on my trash can so throwing away my "bad" work would at least be entertaining. Unfortunately, I was a bad shot, and turned even that into an exercise in frustration as I had to pick up my missed attempts and retry until I made a basket. I couldn't even fail perfectly enough!

I can't be sure what Calder meant by perfection being non-existent for an artist. I believe he meant that eventually a work of art is done, even if the artist feels it could use improvement. I have to disagree with Calder on behalf of one artist who was an extraordinary perfectionist.

Impressionist Claude Monet created nearly 2000 paintings, some of which now sell for more than $100 million each. But he was known to destroy paintings others saw as beautiful works. Monet was angry when his work wasn't good enough in his eyes, and considered his life a failure because of this self-perceived inadequacy as a painter.[14]

Why does this need to always do more, to continue improving something happen? Here's one reason to consider. Perhaps you've heard of the Pareto Principle, sometimes called the 80/20 Rule. It states you get 80% of your results from 20% of your effort or activity. This shows that focusing on what matters most and prioritizing those items will give you a majority of your results.

Brian Tracy wrote about this in his book *Eat That Frog!: 21 Great Ways to Stop Procrastinating and Get More Done in Less Time.* While the book focuses on procrastination, a topic that comes up regularly when discussing perfectionism, he also writes about prioritizing tasks and tackling the most important ones first. [15] Often, the day's most valuable and important tasks are the most challenging and difficult. Yet, the rewards and payoff when complete are exponentially more significant.

Perfectionists flip this rule on its head. Instead of getting 80% of our results from 20% of our effort, a perfectionist gets 20% of their results from 80% of their effort. This is because we procrastinate on the most important tasks since those are the ones at which we are most likely to *fail.* While exhausting, it's another self-inflicted wound.

Whether in your personal life or on the job, you'll have a tough time getting things done if you don't have some basic time management skills. Most people develop poor time management habits because they want to be everywhere and help people with everything. Perfectionists frequently develop these bad habits because they can't quit improving, so nothing is ever complete. This happens because we set our expectations on an impossible standard, which is often based only in our realities.

We base this standard, the personal expectation, on a set of criteria we decided defines the perfect effort. If I do tasks one, two, three, four, and five, I will see acceptable results. If I then add items L, M, N, O, and P, my results become outstanding, perfect by my definition. The problem with this thought process is that completing tasks one, three and four, along with items M and P, is probably good enough, producing an excellent result. But our need to meet an impossible standard prevents us from seeing excellence, even when it's right in front of us.

In my case, using the previous generic example, I would become so fixated on the five tasks and five items that I would lose sight of excellence, and spend a lot of time, energy and effort coming up short of perfect. I would beat myself up for the work not being good enough, looking for what else I needed to add to it, and I would once again be a failure when I couldn't get there. I'd then hold on to that failure and let it define me in other aspects of life. It would drive procrastination, expectations of and relationships with others, and bring on an unbearable pressure to do more the next time to make up for previous shortcomings.

> "PERFECTION IS ACHIEVED, NOT WHEN THERE IS NOTHING MORE TO ADD, BUT WHEN THERE IS NOTHING LEFT TO TAKE AWAY." — ANTOINE DE SAINT-EXUPERY

But next time I would fall short, looking for what else to add, and I'd be a failure again. I did this repeatedly throughout my life. Perhaps I'd have been better off if I had followed the advice of author Antoine de Saint-Exupery who said, "Perfection is achieved, not when there is nothing more to add, but when there is nothing left to take away."

In today's world, the pressure to be perfect is amplified by society and social media. We feel a need to perfect everything we put out in the world for others to see. I have caught myself editing a social media post, even days or weeks after posting it if I noticed I made a typo or grammatical error. Can't let the world see I made a mistake, that would be embarrassing. There it is again, fear. Fear of being embarrassed in front of the world. No one wants to be featured on a customer or passenger shaming website, and we especially don't want to become a worldwide meme phenomenon because of a mistake or inadequacy. As a result, we need to make it all perfect before it goes out into the world.

Unfortunately, that need for perfection and the pressure it applies causes some of us to experience other diseases or forms of psychological disorders. A study published in the *Journal of Research in Personality* concluded many perfectionists become alcoholics[16]. Multiple studies, including the one by Hewitt and Flett referenced earlier, have shown perfectionism can lead to obsessive/compulsive behaviors, eating disorders, depression, attention challenges, and other addictions. In some cases, it even leads to suicidal thoughts, or worse, attempts. The need to perform to a higher standard drives an obsession with achieving something unachievable, and ultimately creates stress, anxiety, and anger that can be debilitating.

What does this look like in life? A perfectionist has a particular way of doing things, of organizing or arranging their possessions, often in ways that a non-perfectionist sees as ridiculous, obsessive or anal-retentive. The bookshelf is organized alphabetically by author and genre, clothes are arranged by color and style, and their nightstand and desk have things arranged in a specific place and orientation. Whatever you do, don't put a book out of order, hang a shirt incorrectly, or rearrange the desk. Any of those will drive the perfectionist crazy, which I can attest to firsthand!

All you have to do is look at my bookshelves and closet for proof. My library is arranged alphabetically by genre. Leadership and personal growth books here, sci-fi/fantasy over there, finance, quality improvement, human behavior and psychology, biographies and history. They all have a place and an order. Then there are those chosen few, those special books that have a place on my desk. Those are my must-reads, my repeat reads, my life-changing titles.

Sound bad enough? Imagine what happens when I get a new book. My space is mostly full, so it's an agonizing effort to find a place, make sure to retain the alphabetized genre separation, decide if something needs to go, and not dilute the special desk collection. In the past, I've spent hours reorganizing the library to add a single book.

My closet isn't much better. Shirts are sorted by type and color. Oxfords to the left, polos to the right, business logo shirts on the outside of each set, with color groupings that transition from one to the next nicely across the color spectrum. Do you have any idea how hard it is to decide what order to place the various shades of blues and purples in to get the right transition? I do. I've spent hours reordering and rehanging clothes because the transitions from one color to the next weren't right. Now, I have no idea what right is, but I knew my closet wasn't it yet, so I had to try again.

Between the oxfords and the polos hang the dress pants, also properly color grouped and arranged. It doesn't stop there, though, as the drawers follow suit. T-shirts, undershirts, shorts and socks all have a certain way they are folded and stored, with arrangement dictated by color, theme (sports team, patriotic, plain, etc.) or use (public wear versus around the house). By the way, t-shirts are tri-folded across and up, but undershirts fold down the middle and tri-fold up. Please don't try to help, only to make me have to refold them later.

That's life inside the perfection paradox for you. No matter how many ways there are to fold a shirt, the perfectionist finds the one way that's right for them, and no other method will be good enough.

6

IF YOU COULD JUST SEE
THINGS MY WAY

*The man with insight enough to admit his
limitations comes nearest to perfection.*

— Johann Wolfgang von Goethe

Unfortunately, life inside the paradox isn't limited to ourselves. We share the misery with everyone around us. Often perfectionists feel like no one can do things as well as we can, so we hold on to assignments, micromanage, or are overly controlling. Even worse, we may become intolerant of anything that doesn't meet our standards and expectations. Our intolerance sometimes evolves into a "my way or the highway" point of view. We use legions of red pens and become proficient editors, and we become unforgiving of other's "errors." This is what I referred to earlier as other-oriented perfection.

Think for a moment of perfectionism as an addiction. When we think of addiction, we usually think of the damage it does to the addict, but less about the damage to others.

Perfectionism falls into that mold, but in reality, being a perfectionist harms relationships, friendships, careers, and more. People don't want to be around you, the best employees don't want to work for you, and your family, well, at times they just don't want to be.

We think perfection will make us and everyone around us better, but we often end up alienating others, usually without realizing it. Instead, we are viewed as demanding, pushy, unforgiving, or even plain arrogant. According to the great author Leo Tolstoy, "An arrogant person considers himself perfect. This is the chief harm of arrogance. It interferes with a person's main task in life—becoming a better person."

While the unrelenting desire for better was the most powerful manifestation of perfection in my life, my other-oriented perfectionism was the most troubling aspect. For me, things were black or white, win or lose, perfect or failure, or in the case of other people, do it right or don't do it at all.

As you can imagine, I had a tough time building meaningful relationships with people in any setting. I tried my best to be forgiving, hands-off, and supportive, but this is where I took the lessons learned from my parents, bosses and mentors and twisted them into something they were never meant to be.

Much of my career was in government or government-contracted work. I was sick of hearing the phrase "good enough for government work", so I coined a personal motto, "Good Enough Isn't Good Enough." I mentioned earlier that I advanced to supervisory and managerial positions reasonably young, so it was important to me that my reputation as a high achiever was protected. I couldn't let something imperfect go out, or it would reflect poorly on me. As a result, getting good enough took on some ugly forms at work and home. Here's what that pursuit of perfection looked like in my life.

Let's start with work first, because that's where work usually ranked for me. There were three main areas where projecting perfection on my staff came into play over the years. Those were assignments, presentations, and performance evaluations.

Handing out assignments was a challenge in many ways. I hated to do it because I always worried the person I assigned something to wouldn't do as good a job as I would have. Of course, I had to give assignments out since I didn't have the capacity to do everything myself, but my staff knew what to expect. Work product had to be reviewed before going out, and if I reviewed an assignment, they knew it was coming back with red all over it. Several times, until it was perfect. My administrative assistants used to order extra boxes of red pens because I went through so many of them. I'm not proud to say that, but it's true.

The same went for presentations. You expected to run it by me several times first while I picked apart your slides, corrected every little "mistake," questioned every fact or figure, and asked for revisions that would make it similar to what I would have presented. You know, perfect. In my mind, this came from the way I learned to prepare for a presentation. Things like knowing your material better than anyone else in the room, and being prepared for the most likely questions to answer them during your presentation were necessities.

Earlier I mentioned how well one of my bosses, Pam, had prepared us for presentations and meetings. This is how I warped that lesson from being prepared to being overbearing. I'm pretty sure Pam didn't teach me to make my staff do it my way, but that's where my perfectionistic mind took the lesson.

Perhaps the harshest projection of all was in the area of performance expectations and evaluations. I had high expectations and felt I communicated them well, but I wasn't good at communicating what I thought of the progress along the way. If you didn't meet my performance expectations, annual review time was going to be painful. Can you imagine working for a perfectionist, knowing your performance review was coming soon? That had to be horrifying!

I was never afraid of giving low scores or creating improvement plans, but I wasn't afraid of giving a good evaluation when it was earned either. A stand-out example of this happened in the early 2000s. I gave an annual review to an employee I promoted during the year. Kelly was a top performer and one of my most reliable staff members. He was a superstar, so I promoted him, even though I had to twist his arm to accept the advancement.

> CAN YOU IMAGINE WORKING FOR A PERFECTIONIST, KNOWING YOUR PERFORMANCE REVIEW WAS COMING SOON? THAT HAD TO BE HORRIFYING!

We met to discuss his annual performance review, and at the end, he seemed disappointed. When I asked him what he thought of his review, he said it was the worst he'd received in all his years at the agency. My honest response was that it was one of the best reviews I had ever given. It was a sobering lesson in differing perceptions, but one I didn't learn until many years later. Or so I thought.

Recently, during the writing of this book, I was reminded of how easy it is for the addiction to rear its ugly head and cause a perfectionist to relapse into old patterns. I grew increasingly critical of some members of my staff for not living up to my performance expectations as project and construction managers. Why couldn't they get the job done correctly? The situation was becoming unbearable due to my frustration with their inability to perform, while simultaneously, they grew frustrated with my lack of properly communicating my expectations and standards.

I thought I had done so, but what I actually did was rely on an assistant to deliver incomplete and insufficient messages. Then, due to my unhappiness with the situation, I fell into my old habits by default instead of addressing the situation. Fortunately, a team member spoke up about my shortcomings, and we addressed the issues head-on, starting the process of putting everything back in order. It was a current example to me showing how easy it is to slip back into old ways.

Projecting a need for perfection wasn't reserved for work; I also shared it with my family. Recall from my story of self-inflicted perfectionism that my folks never put pressure on me to be a top performer at school, only to do the best I could do. I told my kids the same thing, to do the best they could at school, but I expected top grades. They never heard me say it, but they knew. How? Earn an award or get named to the honor roll and I hung it up on the wall outside my office at work for the world to see. Later, when social media arrived, I broadcast it to the world. Get a B, that's nice, honey. Thank goodness I finally broke this pattern for our younger girls, but our eldest endured a tough time with this.

Household chores were another challenge. Loading the dishwasher seemed like an easy enough chore—until I saw how they completed the task. It took mere seconds to look into the machine and figure out they did it "wrong." If I completely reloaded it, I could get a couple more glasses in there.

Yardwork? I'll take care of the grass, and the bushes, and the weeds, and everything else too. I told them it was therapeutic for me, but in reality, we all knew a part of it was because I didn't trust them to get it right. I mean, I did everything perfectly so why couldn't everyone else? How do you think this affected their willingness to do any chores around the house? Yep, not too excited.

The reality is performing brain surgery needs to be perfect, but giving a presentation about asset management or loading the dishwasher wasn't worth straining the relationship between me and my work team or family like it did.

7

OH, THE THINGS I DO FOR YOU

*Perfectionists demand perfection from
themselves first and foremost.*

— Joyce Meyer

One thing perfectionists excel at is providing exceptional service to others. Just ask, and we'll let you know what a great job we've done for you. Okay, maybe it isn't that bad; after all, even a perfectionist can be humble. But we are great at thinking we're providing exceptional service to everyone else by seeking perfection.

For example, no matter how well things are going, or how happy everyone else is with progress, a perfectionist can always identify what might go wrong. We see it as identifying the potential pitfalls or being realistic, but others often see this as the perfectionist being a Negative Nelly or an eternal pessimist.

Merriam-Webster's Dictionary defines a realist as a person who recognizes what is real or possible in a particular situation, or one who accepts and deals with things as they are. It defines a pessimist as a person inclined to emphasize adverse aspects, conditions, and possibilities or to expect the worst possible outcomes. While these definitions are clearly different, a perfectionist doesn't recognize the differences in themselves. A perfectionist will often refer to their pessimistic projection as a "reality check." I know I've used that description myself more times than I can count over the years.

How is it that a perfectionist sees their realism as a positive, yet others see it as a negative? In all honesty, I always thought my reality checks were a positive thing, and I was doing everyone a favor by expressing those thoughts and opinions. That made me optimistic, right? I was providing a great service by preparing my team, daughters, or whomever I was dealing with for the worst-case result, not because I necessarily expected it, but so they wouldn't be disappointed if it happened. After all, the Eagle Scout in me always tried to be prepared.

Maybe I subconsciously thought whatever we were doing would turn out badly because my perfectionism said so, but most times that wasn't the expressed thought. The unfortunate result of this approach was the loss of enthusiasm or demoralization of the team at best, and the creation of a self-fulfilling prophecy at worst. Somehow, I thought this was good?

Even when we get past the reality checks and the potential pitfalls, perfectionists see all those little mistakes no one else sees. The thing is, sometimes they aren't mistakes at all, just personal preference on the part of the perfectionist who can't get past their need to cast everything in their image. Other times it might be an honest mistake, but a trivial thing when viewed in light of the larger issue at hand. This can lead to embarrassing encounters for everyone involved.

I previously shared my need to review, revise and overprepare my staff in the workplace, but what about those times when it wasn't my team from whom I sought performance? Several years ago, the agency I worked for was looking for an asset management application we could implement to keep track of physical assets, inventory and maintenance work orders. These systems are complex and detailed, often encompassing a combination of multiple databases, geographic information systems, scheduling and communication components.

We invited several different vendors to give a presentation of their solution. This was a chance for them to put their best foot forward in an attempt to win a big contract. During one of the presentations, a slide appeared on the screen with a typographical error in one of the words. I noticed it right away, and my mind registered *error* while I tuned out whatever valuable information was being presented.

My boss at the time, who was every bit the perfectionist I was, actually stopped the presenter to point out the error. At the time I didn't think anything of it because I noticed the typo too. Looking back on it now I see how this "helpful" action was not only not helpful, it was unnecessary and probably more embarrassing than anything else. This company was competing for a six-figure contract, telling us about their capabilities and why we should pick them, and we point out an insignificant typo. What on earth did it matter? It was a little mistake that no one noticed, except the two perfectionists in the crowd.

Why do we notice those little things and feel compelled to bring it to people's attention? The short answer is we think we are helping. When that typo popped up on the screen, everything else went dark. I didn't hear what the presenter was saying or see anything else on that slide, all I saw was the typo. Immediately my mind said I needed to tell them about it to help them. I mean really, who wouldn't want to know they had a mistake in their presentation? Then they could correct it, and I would have helped them out.

Too bad my boss was faster and got the credit for being helpful, right? The vendor was gracious and thanked my boss for pointing it out to them, but I'm guessing they didn't feel the helpfulness later after they left the room and discussed how things had gone.

The reality is that not everyone shares our expectations for perfection. While we think everything must be flawless all the time, others believe they need to do well enough to get the job done, or like in the example above, to win the contract. Not everyone wants to live up to the same standards a per-fectionist self-imposes, and if you try to force those standards on them, you quickly become disliked, disrespected, and resented. Your work may be perfect, but your relationships defi-nitely won't be.

> NOT EVERYONE WANTS TO LIVE UP TO THE SAME STANDARDS A PERFECTIONIST SELF-IMPOSES, AND IF YOU TRY TO FORCE THOSE STANDARDS ON THEM, YOU QUICKLY BECOME DISLIKED, DISRESPECTED, AND RESENTED.

This aspect of perfec-tionism doesn't apply only to work; it can be projected into personal relationships in a damaging way. An interesting example is in the Hallmark Christmas movie *A Christmas Detour*. Sorry all you he-men out there, yes, I watch them.

The female lead, played by Candace Cameron Bure, has a list of 75 traits of the perfect guy. Her fiancé has most but not all of them, and throughout the film, she struggles to convince herself, and everyone else, that marrying him is the right thing.

Of course, it's a Hallmark movie, so she ends up falling for the guy she just met and dumping the near-perfect fiancé for the new man. Ultimately, she invested a lot of time and energy into an imperfect relationship by projecting her image of the perfect guy onto someone who couldn't live up to her expectations. When she finally realized this, and let go of her unrealistic expectations, she found happiness with an imperfect man.

That may be the movies, but how often do we hear about a similar situation playing out in real life? We see people on social media or dating sites using filters and doing everything they can to look amazing, so they can attract someone who is also doing everything they can to look larger than life. There are even services to help you create a profile that will attract your most desired matches. Wanting to attract the perfect partner is fine, but how far do we take it?

My wife and I met on an online dating site where we both were matched and went on dates with other people before connecting. While we met some quality people who weren't our matches, we also encountered people who completely misrepresented themselves to appear better than they were in person—sorry, not interested. Authenticity is much better than false perfection.

Once the connection is made, and a relationship begins, the real issues with perfectionism can come into play. If one person wants to improve their partner, they sometimes do things to encourage the partner to act or behave differently. When it's a perfectionist doing the encouraging, they can often feel superior or more valuable. That can lead to jealousy and anger because "the things I'm doing for you" are not being reciprocated or appreciated.

Romantic relationships don't have exclusive rights to feelings of superiority. As a father of four daughters, I had plenty of opportunities to feel like my perfect parenting was under-appreciated. One of the biggest areas of conflict centered around chores and helping around the house. The girls didn't like doing chores, and I wanted them to do more. I frequently reminded them how much rent, utilities, cell phone, and insurance they didn't have to pay, and all I asked was for them to do the dishes, vacuum, or dust. For me, it became more than a dad asking his kids to help around the house. It became an argument about how much I did for them, and why couldn't they appreciate me enough to do what I wanted them to do.

I even helped them by reviewing their work, then redoing it to show them how to do it better. I mentioned before that my favorite example was to reload the dishwasher to demonstrate how better organization could get more items into the machine.

The idea of asking them to help out in return for our providing for them was fair, but notice how it became about me? I expected them to do it like I would, and thought I was helping them by showing them how much better they could be. In reality, all I did was alienate them and create a situation where they preferred to let me do the chores myself.

Homework time became another challenge in our home, especially math homework. As an engineer, math comes naturally to me and is one of my strong points. Calculating sales tax, discounts, tips, and more in my head almost instantly is a breeze. For my girls, not so much. So why couldn't they appreciate the help I gave them? I taught them all the ways I knew to solve a math problem and even showed them how dumb the "new math" method their teachers were telling them to use was. Homework often turned into a cryfest for them and more frustration for me. Having survived all four of them, though I'm sure they would all tell you they survived me, I now know I let my perfectionistic tendencies interfere with my parenting tenderness.

Think this is limited to family relationships? Try being a perfectionist on a sports team. When things are going well, and the team is winning, no problem. But when things go south and the losing streak sets in, the bitterness rears its ugly head. The perfectionist feels they are carrying the load, the only one doing their part and never making a mistake. Why can't the rest of the team play as well so we can win again? If you've ever seen that come out in a post-game interview, you know how arrogant that player looks to everyone. They come off as egotistical, ungrateful. Call it what you want, but it's not a good look.

That's how it goes in perfectionist relationships. Everything is about you, the perfectionist, not the other person. When you're frustrated, everything wrong is the other person's fault because they don't appreciate your contributions. As a result, you alienate others and sabotage those relationships. It happened around me every day. The problem was I couldn't see it happening.

PART 3

PROGRESS—
GETTING TO
GOOD ENOUGH

8

THE PARADOX REVEALED

Nothing is perfect. Life is messy. Relationships are complex.
Outcomes are uncertain. People are irrational.

— Hugh Mackay

For perfectionists, recovery doesn't begin as an acknowledgement of a problem, but more of a sobering realization of what we have unwittingly done to ourselves and others. Our constant pursuit of perfection eventually leads to frustration, feelings of inadequacy and being exposed as an imposter, and the need to cover for ourselves with a mask of perfection. Only when we admit the causes of our addiction, the results we have realized, and the ways we have covered for our self-perceived shortcomings, can the struggle of undoing begin. But doing that can be easier said than done.

For me, the realization came the night of September 23, 2014, which I now fondly call my perfection revelation date. I participated in a coaching program called *Dream Job Bootcamp* and was on a group coaching call with Kary Oberbrunner and about 25 people I hardly knew at that time, many of whom have become friends since then. That night was a sobering phone call, full of tears as my reality hit me. I realized I wasn't perfect; I was hiding behind a mask of perfection to fool myself into avoiding the pain of believing I wasn't good enough, of the fear of being found out, of the terrifying thought that I was a failure.

For approximately 30 minutes the rest of the group listened in as Kary and I talked about my past, my beliefs, and my struggles. I admitted to my tendency to overanalyze everything in attempts to achieve perfection, to my need to counteract the long-running perception of government performance being substandard, and to my need for professionalism translating into a requirement for nothing ever to be wrong. Kary answered with examples and counterpoints that made me dig deep and think, but more importantly, made me admit I was telling myself a story.

Throughout the conversation (a transcript is included in the appendices) Kary helped me discover how deeply ingrained my feelings of inadequacy were. I also realized I spent the majority of life programming myself with limiting beliefs that hindered me from accomplishing the things I told him were important to me. Perhaps the most revealing part of the conversation, though, was in Kary's closing observations.

He told me I was addicted to "ideal," and asked me a straightforward question; if I couldn't grant myself grace, how could I grant it to anyone else? Family members, coworkers, employees, and friends. The people I needed to achieve my dreams were being repelled from me because I had "ideal addict" plastered across my forehead. Why would people want to help me when my standards and expectations were unachievable? Not only was my learning model not serving me, it was alienating the people in my life.

Kary assigned me the task of posting in the cohort's Facebook group three times a day for two weeks about a situation when I had an urge to be ideal or perfect, but allowed good enough to be good enough. He told me to try new things, and asked me to start with the smallest thing I could think of.

I struggled to answer, so Kary asked about the last time I was hard on someone. In an incident earlier that same day, I asked an employee to update our director about some work we completed. The employee gave the update, and the director was satisfied, but I wasn't because the report wasn't as thorough as I would have provided. I expressed my disappointment in the quality of the report and tried to correct the employee. The problem was he didn't need correction because his report was good enough.

Ouch. There it was. The paradox revealed. That's when the tears flowed, and my life began to change. Everything mentioned in the previous chapters of this book was brought to the light of day for the first time.

> "I'M A PERFECTIONIST. SOMETIMES I HAVE TO REMIND MYSELF THAT IT'S OKAY IF THERE ARE FLAWS HERE AND THERE." —TYRA BANKS

Over the next couple of weeks, I worked hard to complete the assignment Kary gave me. I have no idea if my employees or family noticed the things I let go, but I did. It was painful but worth it. Model and television personality Tyra Banks said "I'm a perfectionist. Sometimes I have to remind myself that it's okay if there are flaws here and there." This sentiment perfectly sums up what I was going through. Each day I reminded myself to let things go because they were good enough.

That conversation started a multi-year journey of self-discovery, struggle, growth, and rebirth as a new person. I spent an incredible amount of time and energy trying to be perfect, all the while thinking perfection would protect me. If I was perfect, I could avoid the pain of judgment, shame, and blame. Now I had to learn how to live in an imperfect world—my imperfect world.

I discovered how exhausting and painful it was pursuing the messages in my head saying I was never good enough, wondering what would people think, or thinking something could be done so much better. Those messages weren't just mine, though. The world often capitalizes on people's weaknesses and addictions without us knowing it, and perfectionism is no exception.

Here's an example that recently jumped out at me. Earlier I mentioned I was a shooter as a youth. At age 16, on my way to winning the junior trapshooting championship for my city, I had to hit more target clays out of 200 than anyone else. There were special awards for streaks, and I hit 189 out of 200, at one point running off almost 75 without a miss. As a small-bore rifle target shooter, I reached sharpshooter grade four, and was able to group three shots under a quarter from 25 yards. Not perfect results in either case, but pretty good.

While I don't shoot much today, I still read *American Rifleman* magazine from time to time. I saw an advertisement in a recent issue that would have been ideal for me back then, before I gained an awareness of my addiction. It was for a scope, a type of sight that looks like a telescope mounted on the top of a rifle. The headline said, "Built by perfectionists for perfectionists," and the text in the ad used words like absolute precision, brilliant clarity, and extreme durability.[17] They knew exactly how to capture the mind, and wallet, of a perfectionist with that ad, using words that reaffirm the perfection of the scope and the user's need for nothing less than that.

British comic Rowan Atkinson said, "I've always believed perfectionism is more of a disease than a quality. I do try to go with the flow, but I can't let go." Although I came to view my perfectionism as more of an addiction than a disease, as I examined my affliction, I quit telling myself that if I wasn't perfect, I was a bad person. That if, or more likely when, I failed at something, I was unworthy, or people won't like or respect me. That it was okay to deviate from the plan and go with the flow.

It is sobering to realize something you've held as a truth for most of your life is not one at all. The beauty is that it's also freeing. I accepted that perfection is a target, not a destination. No matter how hard any of us try, we will never arrive there; no matter how smart we are, we won't find it. It can't be bought, and you can't give or receive it as a gift.

Perfection is an illusion for the delusional to chase, and I was done being delusional. Now, with the paradox revealed, it was time to reclaim my life.

9

BECOMING WORTHY

The thing that is really hard, and really amazing, is giving up on being perfect and beginning the work of becoming yourself.

— Anna Quindlen

Revealing the perfection paradox was a huge step for me, but how to overcome the challenges of perfectionism and learn to live the life I really wanted was another story. How could I embrace imperfection in a world I had conditioned myself to believe demanded perfection? Making a change this drastic would be a challenge, but I decided during that phone call it was time for the change to occur. Sitting on the sidelines, waiting and overthinking, wasn't going to work anymore, and neither was hoping for some miracle to make life different. This was going to take effort.

In addiction recovery programs, professionals say the first step is acknowledging you have a problem. That becomes a bit of a problem for perfectionists because there isn't a built-in next step. There is no 12-step program or inpatient recovery center for perfectionists. We have to find other ways to control our demons. You might choose to work with a coach, a therapist, or a circle of trusted and valued friends, or maybe you have the strength and discipline to tackle it yourself. Whichever method you choose, the process of letting go will be painful and will require commitment, perseverance, and most importantly, granting yourself grace.

With the severity of my addiction, I needed a hybrid approach that included all these methods and more. I needed to reassess my situation, reflect on my past behaviors and beliefs, and think about my purpose in life. All deep subjects, sure, but the reality is I had to go there to get here. And to go there, the first thing I had to do was forgive myself. As strange as that sounds, the truth is I was no harder on anyone else than I was on myself.

Granting myself the grace to be imperfect was critical, and was the key to unlocking everything else. Allowing myself to be free of being perfect gave self-reflection and exploration permission to be honest; which revealed three key aspects of the perfection paradox that dominated my struggle. Sure, there are probably many more than three, but these interrelated beliefs were my keys. I was convinced I wasn't good enough; I was certain people would discover I was an imposter; and I was afraid of failing.

Perfection equates to worthiness for a perfectionist, and that need to be worthy often makes us believe we are never attractive, smart, extraordinary, talented, popular, promoted, admired, or accomplished enough. These lack of self-worth feelings drove most other aspects of my perfection addiction.

My feelings of unworthiness caused me to doubt my skills and abilities, and to procrastinate, then regret, the opportunities I missed because of my doubt and delay. Sometimes I couldn't even get started for fear of not being good enough, thus making me a failure once again. It was a brutal, self-feeding spiral that caused anxiety, sadness, and even self-loathing. I had to overcome these feelings of unworthiness and learn how to believe in myself.

Belief in yourself must come from within, but support from others is never a bad thing. It's critical to find the right support system. While friends and family can be great encouragers, you need a network of people who will have your back and encourage you, not blow smoke up your backside. When Kary told me he believed in me, and I should borrow his belief until my own was strong enough, it was a heavy weight lifted off my chest. His belief opened the door to several critical realizations.

We are all different, so your version of success may look and feel different than mine, and that's okay. In fact, that's good, because each of us is a different person with different needs, wants, and dreams. None of us is more or less important or worthy than the other. Every day when you wake up, you should be excited about the day ahead, not dreading it.

In his book *Discover Your Sweet Spot*, Scott Fay says if you don't like how your typical Monday goes, you should create a better Monday.[18] In my case it wasn't so much a day that was the problem; it was that I didn't like my sense of self-worth, so I needed to create a better one. I deserved to find my success, purpose, and joy in life, but I had to accept imperfection to do so. That meant taking inventory of some challenging aspects of life.

I started looking at my relationships, or more specifically, who I was spending time with and how that served me. Did the people I associated with encourage me, make me happy and lift me up, or were they holding me back? You may have heard the saying that you are the sum of the five people with whom you spend the most time. Well, I had to make some tough choices about who I was spending time with and implement changes in my inner circle.

That meant distancing myself from some long-time friends who I needed to grow away from if I was going to change my thoughts and actions. At the same time, I needed to strengthen my relationships with supportive people who believed in me, and vice versa. This required connecting on a deeper level with friends and acquaintances who I knew could develop into relationships that served us both because of shared values, characteristics and beliefs. People who would talk me out of my self-doubt and mean it.

Relationships don't only mean friends and acquaintances. Often our worst critics are our family. Family members will often attempt to talk you out of trying something new, or will say your idea won't work so you shouldn't even try it. Don't get me wrong, they are well-meaning and believe they genuinely have your best interest at heart, but for someone who already has feelings of unworthiness and self-doubt, that lack of encouragement and support can be crushing.

I discovered how lucky I was in this regard, as my family was never discouraging. They were exactly what I needed in that they were supportive, but weren't afraid to call me out. What I realized was I didn't listen to them very well, though, so I had to learn to appreciate and accept their input regularly.

Changing your inner circle can be a scary thought at first. Initially, it seems as if you are deciding to eliminate friends and family from your life. In reality, all you are doing is refining to whom you give the most influence in your life. When you think about it, you can't really quit your family, even if you want to. They will always be family. Modifying who you spend your time with doesn't mean you are choosing who is or isn't a friend, or which cousin is your favorite. It merely shifts how much time and space each is going to get from now on. That was a key realization for me in these choices.

After working through the relationship changes I needed to make, it was time to look at how I thought about past achievements. I had to define my worthiness in a new way, changing the negative stories I had fed myself for years. The key point here is if you've been successful at something, no matter how large or small, it's important to celebrate that.

Instead of criticizing myself for being an inadequate Eagle Scout, I reframed how I viewed my experience. I realized it's not about the rank, whether I earned Palms or not, or even about the accomplishment, but rather about casting my belief about the achievement in a new light. I shifted my perspective from disappointment to pride. Now I carry an Eagle Scout challenge coin in my pocket as the symbol of a meaningful achievement instead of an ideal I didn't live up to.

Using the same approach, I took on a slew of demons. I relaxed and let things go, granting myself grace for little mistakes. I got over being overweight as a lifelong sentence; I've now lost well over 100 pounds and am keeping it off as of the time I wrote this. Instead of putting all my credentials on display so others would know my value, I took nearly all the letters off my business cards and email signatures. I kept the credentials to myself as a reminder of the knowledge and expertise I can use to benefit myself and others.

This same approach works with any misplaced belief about an accomplishment. It's about overcoming the negative viewpoint and reframing it positively. Call it anything that works for you—refocusing, changing your perspective, modifying your mindset, or viewing the issue through a different lens. However you phrase it, even if the only result is you learn you don't want to repeat something, that's a good result.

Decide to celebrate your success, no matter how big or small. Did you graduate from school? That's a huge success, no matter what grade you got in "that" class. Did you get your driver's license? Who cares how many questions you missed on the test? If you need to get down to the very smallest success, that's okay. For some of us getting out of bed this morning was an accomplishment.

Happiness and success don't require perfection; you need to look beyond the imperfections and appreciate each day, each action, each win, for what it is. I've found this simple act of practicing gratitude resulted in a powerful shift in my thinking about achievements, big or small.

Our feelings of unworthiness often stem from the comparison trap I mentioned earlier. All comparison does is breed more doubt, so quit comparing yourself to others. The reality is we don't know what anyone else's journey looks like, what struggles they do or don't have, or how authentic their projection is. And truthfully, most of them don't care about you.

> YOUR SELF-WORTH DOESN'T DEPEND ON THE APPROVAL OF OTHERS—IT'S CALLED SELF-WORTH FOR A REASON.

There's a saying that when you're 20 you care what everyone thinks, when you're 40 you stop caring what everyone thinks, and when you're 60 you realize no one was ever thinking about you in the first place. I say we shouldn't wait for 60 to make that realization. Your self-worth doesn't depend on the approval of others—it's called self-worth for a reason. The perception you have of yourself depends solely on your own opinions. When you are happy with who you are, flaws and all, you are less likely to need everything to be perfect; you're okay with making mistakes, with the way you look, and the situation you're in.

Besides feelings of unworthiness, I also dealt with a paralyzing case of imposter syndrome. A powerful affliction affecting many people, imposter syndrome is common in perfectionists. While everyone suffers from self-doubt on occasion, a perfectionist with impostor syndrome feels this way all the time, harboring debilitating self-doubt that fuels constant anxiety and worry of not living up to expectations, whether our own or those of others.

An underlying cause of this is setting standards that are far too rigorous, or what some might call setting the bar too high. As a result, we doubt we have the skills or abilities to do something competently, even if we do. We think we are faking it or underperforming, and that anyone who believes we are capable is either dishonest with us or doesn't know anything. Those unreasonable standards are often subconsciously set, so we sabotage ourselves to confirm our self-defined lack of expertise by failing to achieve the expected results. If we do achieve them, we believe we were lucky, in the right place at the right time, or that we should have done more and those standards were set too low. We can't possibly accept the success as genuine or deserved. It's a no-win situation.

It may be hard to believe, but denying success can breed it. Those same feelings of unworthiness and of being an imposter can become fuel for even greater levels of success if we let them. Barbara Corcoran of Shark Tank fame said, "Thank God you doubt yourself because the one thing I have learned that is true of every single person who is exceptional in whatever they are doing is self-doubt. Without it, you become big-headed, arrogant. The curse of being competent is self-doubt, because competence rides on your own self-doubt. It's the edge of doubt that makes you a performer in anything you do."[19]

In my case, my feelings of unworthiness fueled by imposter syndrome driven self-doubt translated to fear of being discovered as a fraud. The anxiety arising from this fear can be overwhelming. Renowned poet and civil rights activist Maya Angelou once said "I have written eleven books, but each time I think, uh oh, they're going to find out now. I've run a game on everybody, and they're going to find me out."

Imposter syndrome isn't easy to overcome, but the discomfort it causes isn't a set of imprisoning shackles either. You can override the uncomfortable feelings to do what you want to do, but it requires you to address your past behaviors and natural tendencies. Acknowledge that imposter syndrome is a challenge in your life, and recognize the issues it causes—how does it limit you, make you unhappy, or cost you money?

Outwardly others may see you as good, successful, or having it all together, but to people with impostor syndrome, our public persona is a facade, hiding flaws and imperfections. Getting past the feeling of not being good enough required me to believe my inner circle and support system, accept I deserved my accomplishments, and adopt a different mindset where success replaced luck. Success doesn't happen through luck; it only happens at the intersection of opportunity and preparedness.

The last piece of accepting my worthiness involved my fear of failure. Because of the unrealistically high standards perfectionists believe we need to live up to, we constantly worry about disappointing others and have a substantial fear of failure, which for us means being seen as one. This fear of failure, or of being a failure, is a major contributor to perfectionism, which Kary Oberbrunner often says, "is just fear in disguise." If you feel you've been stuck in the same place for a long time, you're most likely afraid of failure. This fear causes us to procrastinate because you can't fail if you don't try. Unfortunately, you can't accomplish anything either.

Can you imagine what life would be like if Thomas Edison had been afraid of failing? Edison made over 10,000 failed attempts inventing the incandescent light bulb before succeeding. If fear of failure had affected him like it does a perfectionist, you'd be reading this book by candlelight. Edison didn't see it as failing at all. He said, "I have not failed 10,000 times. I have not failed once. I have succeeded in proving that those 10,000 ways will not work. When I have eliminated the ways that will not work, I will find the way that will work."[20]

Interestingly, when it comes to fear among perfectionists, the fear of success is as strong as the fear of failure. While that might sound ridiculous, it's a common issue. Success carries a different set of burdens; you become more visible and have more responsibility when you're successful. Maybe you will be seen as an influencer, a thought leader, or a subject matter expert and as a result, you become the victim of higher expectations in the future.

In my case, the fear of being considered a subject matter expert in my field was terrifying. To me, that meant an even higher level of expectation I had to live up to, with more eyes than ever focused on me while waiting for me to screw it up. This could become debilitating if you don't do what I finally did and accept that you deserve the status, you've earned the right to be there, and you have everything it takes to deliver and meet those expectations. This was incredibly empowering for me, as once I accepted my value in this area, I gained confidence and became a more valuable resource to others.

Perhaps the most significant part of the fear of failure is worrying about what others will think of us when we fail. This flows from the mindset that anyone cares about what you're doing to begin with. When things fall apart and don't work out the way you planned, you take it personally, feeling less of a person, or that you dropped the ball. Unfortunately, the more you think other people are obsessed about your failure, the worse your failures become. Why? Because you're less likely to try again. You get knocked down, and you stay down because you're too afraid of how people will view your failure. Then you create a variety of reasons and excuses not to try again.

Can I let you in on a little secret? Everybody fails—all of us. People make mistakes, do things we shouldn't, make wrong decisions, and sometimes do everything right, but the results aren't there. Regardless of how you define it, everybody fails. It's better to do something imperfectly than to do nothing flawlessly; Edison figured this out early on, but it took me a little longer.

It's one thing to assume people will have some level of concern for you when you're down on your luck. That's okay; it's healthy and the way it should be. That's why you have a support network, your carefully selected inner circle. But assuming people care and obsess about your failures is nothing less than a form of self-torture.

As spectacular as your failure may be, at the end of the day, everyone has their problems to take care of, their failures to attend to. Sure, some people might sit up and say, "Wow, that's harsh," or "Thank goodness that didn't happen to me," but at the end of the day they move on, and so should you. As George Addair said, "Everything you ever wanted is on the other side of fear."

10

LEARNING TO LIVE INSIDE THE PARADOX

It's not about perfect. It's about effort.
And when you bring that effort every single day,
that's where transformation happens.

— Jillian Michaels

Discovering my addiction and allowing myself permission to be worthy were great accomplishments, but the real challenge sat in learning to live inside the paradox, how to deal with and "control" my perfectionism daily. The starting point was the challenge Kary gave me during that now-infamous call to post in our group about the times I granted myself grace and let something go I previously would have handled differently.

As challenging as that was, imagine living every day knowing you need to let things go to be productive, successful and happy. I was the guy who genuinely believed someone could die if I made a mistake. The reality is there are numerous safety factors figured into engineering design, and there are multiple levels of design and plan checks to make sure we catch all the big mistakes before they ever get to the construction site. It was highly unlikely a mistake I made would cause someone to die. Not impossible, but highly unlikely. I needed to turn that mindset into a more positive, productive, success-oriented one. Some of the tips and tools I used to do that follow in this chapter.

As a perfectionist, what can you do to overcome procrastination? The number one thing is to get started. Todd Beamer said, "Let's Roll." Dale Carnegie said, "Inaction breeds doubt and fear. Action breeds confidence and courage. If you want to conquer fear, do not sit home and think about it. Go out and get busy." Thomas Jefferson said, "Do you want to know who you are? Don't ask. Act! Action will delineate and define you." Nike says, "Just Do It." And my personal favorite, Robin Williams, in the movie *The Dead Poet's Society,* said, "Carpe Diem. Seize the day boys, seize the day."

Remember, imperfect action beats perfect inaction every time. Once you get going, you will build momentum, which will encourage you to keep going and help fight the stuck and stressed feeling that causes delay. If "just do it" isn't your speed, I get it. My perfection addiction was so deeply ingrained that even with the progress I've made overcoming it, I still have to deal with those over-organized, over-analytical tendencies. When I seize the day, I think about what my seizing looks like and how it will work. Here's a method I use to turn just doing it and seizing the day into a positive way to prevent procrastination.

To start, break the project or assignment into several small tasks, not worrying about the details, but focusing on dividing it into what intuitively seems like logical parts.

Organize those parts by prioritizing them and listing them in sequential order. Don't spend a lot of time on this, organize the tasks by what makes sense.

Next, give each task a deadline or time limit. This doesn't have to be a detailed schedule with bells and whistles, just guidance on how long to spend or when each task needs to be finished. Notice this says finished, not perfected. Done is the key. You can always come back and edit, update or fine-tune later.

Once you begin a task, eliminate as many distractions as possible. Distractions are nothing more than your mind getting hacked, momentum killers that put you right back on the road to procrastination. You have to become perfectly unhackable.

Turning off notifications on your phone and computer is a great start; the last thing you need is to get thrown off track by a photo of Uncle Joe's dinner or an email saying a long lost relative in some country you've never heard of wants to send you money. If possible, close the door to block out noises or visitors. If you need background noise, play something that works for you but doesn't require focus. Listening to a podcast or having the news on in the background is likely to steal your attention from what you're doing. That's a distraction you don't want. I still struggle with this as I want to have music or the TV on in the background, so I've got some work to do.

Make sure to take breaks while you're working; there's no joy in sitting at a desk or on a computer for hours on end. Take a walk, get some sunlight and fresh air, do mindfulness breathing or movement, or grab a healthy snack. Try to take a short break every hour to keep your attention sharper and your frustration lower. There's a reason high school and college classes are often scheduled for 50-minute durations. My Fitbit vibrates at ten minutes to the hour, every hour, which serves as a great reminder to either get up and move or do some relaxation breathing. A key point here is not to let your breaks turn into an exercise in more distraction and procrastination.

Last but not least, celebrate each accomplishment. After completing the task at hand, reward yourself by allowing a little time to relax and say "good job," or do something you've wanted to do. I've treated myself by taking time to watch a webinar or video for small goal accomplishments, and given myself a day off or purchased a special reward for larger accomplishments. It doesn't matter if you pick one of my examples, or take a break for a movie or meal out with your family. Whatever you choose as long as it's meaningful to you.

While this may seem obvious, the perfectionist pull is so hard that even a simple approach becomes challenging. If a task is something you aren't excited about doing to begin with, then procrastination finds no shortage of allies. You can get past this pull by focusing on how good you will feel when the task is done instead of how much you don't want to do it.

> PERFECTIONISTS WILL PROCRASTINATE UNTIL THE PAIN OF DOING THE TASK AT HAND IS LESS THAN THE PAIN OF NOT DOING IT.

Perfectionists will procrastinate until the pain of doing the task at hand is less than the pain of not doing it. The ironic thing is that by waiting, the pain is far greater than if the task was managed earlier.

Dr Norman Vincent Peale, the author of *The Power of Positive Thinking*, said, "Really happy people are those who have broken the chains of procrastination, those who find satisfaction in doing the job at hand. They're full of eagerness, zest, and productivity. You can be, too."[21] Thanks, Dr Peale, I'm with you!

While writing this chapter, I found a lot of distractions. I may have said "found," but to be honest, I created the distractions, and did so frequently. That is until my wife called me out, telling me to quit procrastinating and get back to work on the book that was so close to being finished. I admitted to her that my fears of not being good enough were creeping in, so I was 'finding' distractions to avoid finishing because I didn't think I could quit trying to fix things. My first draft already underwent multiple self-edits; I sometimes jokingly said, "it's a first draft with about 37 edits to its credit." The relentless pursuit of better, of good isn't good enough, can be stressful and debilitating.

The same pursuit of better preventing me from completing this book also prevented me from getting things done at work and from enjoying life in general. How can you be more productive or enjoy time with family or friends when you're worried about details that aren't significant in the scheme of things? Maybe your detail isn't as extreme as how your shirts are folded (remember, it's in thirds lengthwise, and then in thirds upwards), but whatever it is, you need to have it just right. Oh, the agony of cleaning the house to have friends over for dinner! Has that served you as poorly as it did me?

I'll share a way you can tackle this tendency that worked for me. It's an adaptation of Kurt Lewin's Force Field Analysis, a simple but powerful change management decision-making tool I learned over 25 years ago, but recently began using in this new way.

In a Force Field Analysis, you compare the forces causing change against the forces resisting it by applying weight or value to each force. Then, compare the sum of the forces for and against to determine what change is needed to achieve the desired outcome. In my case, it was about comparing the causes of my need for perfection, the results I was getting, and how that manifested in my life. Here's how I went about it.

Grab a piece of paper, draw a line down the middle from top to bottom, and title the left side 'causes' and the right side 'results.' You can find a fillable template at jeffreyakramer.com/resources. Now answer the following questions, writing down everything you can think of on the 'causes' side.

- When have you been so obsessed with improvement that it made you sick?

- What have you organized over and over again, but still aren't satisfied with the result?

- What drives you crazy when someone changes it?
- What mistake immediately makes you want to trash your work and start over?
- When do you want to redo someone else's work?

Think about your list of causes and what results they have brought about. Have you experienced any of these?

- Excessive weight changes or eating disorders
- Physical illness
- Stressed so much you withdrew from your environment
- Missed family activities or social events while you were busy perfecting
- Been ridiculed for what you were doing when noticed by others
- Been called obsessive or anal-retentive (or worse)
- Miss out on an excellent opportunity, and then regretted it and beat yourself up mentally and emotionally over it
- Alienated people because of your actions

Write them down on the results side, next to the cause it came from if possible. Just as important, if you've experienced positive results write those down too. Once finished, set your pen down and review your lists.

If they're anything like mine were, it's pretty overwhelming to see. I've been there, so I get it. You need to reduce those negative and damaging effects in your life, and the way to do that is to get rid of the causes that generate more negative results than positive ones. At a minimum, reframe the results so they're less damaging. Quit worrying about a book being in the wrong spot—it's still in your library where you can find it.

Having a hard time deciding in what color order your shirts should be hung? Hang them up; they'll wear the same. Allow yourself to make a typo on a social media post and not go back to edit it. In the words of Elsa from the Disney movie *Frozen*, "let it go."

Another thing to let go is projecting your need for perfection onto your relationships with others. What relationships have you unknowingly damaged? How can you overcome those feelings of being unappreciated? My family members shouldn't have to be perfect for me to love them; we love each other because of who we are, faults and all. My coworkers and employees don't have to be perfect for us to be successful and produce excellent work. My teammates don't have to play error-free for us to win.

Look for the positive in things rather than the reality in them. I know that sounds odd, but reality lives in a space between positive and negative. If our inclination as perfectionists is to project reality as pessimistic, making a conscious effort to find the positive before we express reality will make us more likely to frame it in a positive light. Instead of looking for what could go wrong, look for all the ways it could go well. Instead of reloading the dishes to get a couple more glasses in the machine, thank your child for doing the dishes. Instead of trying to change your partner to meet your vision of perfect, let them know how much you appreciate them for who they are. Positivity, gratitude and acceptance are a great starting point to overcome the need to fix everyone and everything.

Think about people you may have discouraged, undermined, alienated or plain infuriated over the years by your need for perfection. Do you need to apologize to an employee, teammate, neighbor, coworker, boss, or family member? Before you go any further, reach out to make that apology. They may have forgotten all about it, but you haven't, and the apology is as much for you as it is for them.

That may sound selfish, but trust me, it will free a part of your soul you don't even realize is imprisoned and they will appreciate you for doing it. I've made apologies to my daughters, my wife, former coworkers, and recently even to an employee I was holding to an unreasonable standard. Here are some steps that may help with repairing relationships.

Take the pressure off your kids. Healthy child development needs reasonable expectations and opportunities for unstructured play, not regimented imprisonment. Kids can enjoy swimming without trying to set Olympic records or play an instrument without joining the local philharmonic orchestra. In the long run, a hard-earned B is worth more than an easy A. Congratulate your child for persisting with their math homework, however long it takes. In a nutshell, praise your kids for pitching in to help, for giving their best effort, and for showing quality character. The results will come, and the lessons will be learned, as long as you don't push them to the point of no return.

When it comes to relationships, perfectionism can make you feel like a loser when comparing yourself to others. Turn that around by celebrating other people's successes; I like to tell people that a rising tide lifts all ships. This mindset will enrich your relationships. Similarly, it's hard to go through life feeling like you have to hide your weaknesses. Sharing your challenges with others may help you find more support, and gives other people the freedom to do the same.

Vulnerability is a powerful thing. When I embraced being vulnerable and authentic, began sharing my struggles, challenges, and successes, and openly acknowledging and celebrating others reaching goals I was struggling with myself, it had an enormously positive impact on my outlook and relationships.

That same approach can help you be more inclusive and accepting of others. As a perfectionist, negative self-talk isn't uncommon, and it can make you apprehensive about criticism from others. Face this head-on by asking for feedback. People usually appreciate being asked for their input, and you'll get valuable information far more often than not. It helps to grant others a little grace too. Performing surgery needs to be precise, but most things can withstand a little give and take. For example, if your spouse has a different approach to vacuuming than you do, both you and your house will survive if your partner does the vacuuming. I quit worrying about how the dishwasher got loaded, the towels got folded, and the vacuum got run. It was all good enough.

Ease the pressure on yourself and others. By overcoming your perfectionism, you'll enjoy more happiness and have more energy. When you recognize that your happiness comes from within, you'll feel less need to try to control your environment and the behavior of others. Focus on maintaining your peace of mind even when things go wrong or turn out differently from what you expected. When I let all those little things go, I was much happier, and so were the people around me.

Another aspect of easing pressure on yourself is learning to accept failure is about the activity or event, not the person. Reframe the idea of failure and realize that it's one of many possible results, and provides an opportunity for growth. You can choose to learn from that result and apply it to your next attempt; expect to fail like Edison did.

James Dyson created 5,126 vacuums that didn't work before one that did, and the Dyson vacuum is now the market leader.[22] Harland Sanders' chicken recipe was rejected by 1,009 restaurants. You've probably heard of the one that said yes, KFC. Stephen King's first book, *Carrie*, was rejected by 30 publishers before one accepted it; he's now sold nearly 400 million books.[20] The more often you fail, the faster you'll reach your goals. Don't let an irrational fear become an obstacle to success.

Embracing imperfection allows you to examine your fear of failure and mistakes and why they are holding you back.

It lets you see what's really behind your fears. Here's a simple process to examine your fear's root cause.

Name the basic fear—not fear of failure but what you're afraid will happen if you fail. Keep drilling down for detail until you get to the root of the fear. Are you afraid of being laughed at or not being liked? Why? What's really behind the fear? Remember, life isn't a high school popularity contest; our lives are ours to be lived. Define what would actually happen if you failed? Would it cause a major catastrophe or health problem? I'm guessing probably not, which is what I came to discover.

Dealing with your past and your tendencies is a huge step in the right direction. However, there are a present set of challenges to clear up, too. When you've approached the world a certain way for an extended period of time, like demanding perfection for 40-plus years as I did, you develop habits. Those habits won't vanish by resolving past issues. The first step only sets the stage for change to happen.

My habits were exposed in the perfection revelation phone call I mentioned in chapter eight. Many experts say it takes 21 days to create a new habit, but in his book *The 5 AM Club*, Robin Sharma describes a 66-day process that includes breaking the old habit followed by creating and institutionalizing the new one.[23] In my case, breaking old habits took several years, and I'm still working on installing new ones.

> CREATING NEW HABITS IS HARD WORK, BUT OVERCOMING IMPOSTER SYNDROME REQUIRES NEW HABITS.

Habits, like a New Year's resolution, an exercise or diet plan, a financial savings plan, and so many others, are easy to quit. Creating new habits is hard work, but overcoming imposter syndrome requires new habits, so commit to following through and ridding yourself of the mask you've been wearing.

Part of my habit change process was becoming consistent with the changes I wanted to make, which meant I needed to adopt new support mechanisms and tools. There are tons of options out there, so I experimented until I found the ones that worked for me. That's an important point to understand, so think about it like this. When I wanted to lose weight throughout my life, I used a variety of diet plans, but the weight always came back. Until I used Noom. For some reason, Noom was the system that worked for me; I lost 120 pounds and am keeping it off. Does that mean other plans don't work? Absolutely not. Some people do great on those other plans, but for me, my body, and more importantly, my mind, Noom was the one that worked.

Back to those habit changing tools. In the books I read and courses I attended, there were consistently repeated keys to success: journaling, morning routines, meditation, positive mindset, visualization, and more. To get organized and implement some of these concepts, I identified and adopted a handful of tools that work for me in the way I think and function. That's a key point—as with my weight loss, finding tools that work for you is critical if you want to become perfectly unhackable. I've provided brief descriptions here, but if you want more information on these tools, visit jeffreyakramer. com/resources.

Journaling and meditation are tough for me, but planning, and incorporating an aspect of journaling and reflection into that planning, I could do. Once upon a time, I used the Franklin Planner system but was never consistent. There are dozens upon dozens of planner options out there, but in my search, I discovered the EVO Planner™. EVO has four different planner versions, each with minor content and layout changes based on your brain type as defined by their EVO Brain Type Assessment™.

My brain type, Architect, was a dead-on match for my DISC type C personality and perfectionist tendencies. Better yet, the Architect version of the planner is organized in a way that makes sense to me, focusing on planning and prioritization, but including elements of journaling, gratitude and life balance in a simple and concise way. As a plus, the associated smartphone app has planning and reflection meditations and a focus timer to help you get into flow. Each day you scan your completed daily assessment from your planner to keep a running history of your progress and flow state. Score!

I also wanted a tool to track my thoughts and ideas, and to record quotes, images or statistics I wanted to keep in a place I could access without having to keep a huge notebook or transfer the items from one planner to the next. That's where THINKERS Notebook came in. THINKERS Notebook is similar in concept to Evernote, which I also use, but I find it easier and more flexible and am rapidly moving toward using it exclusively.

I use the notebook pages to capture thoughts, experiment with ideas, draft marketing funnels, etc., then save them to the smartphone app where I can retrieve them from anywhere, or share them with other people whether they use the app or not. You can easily save scans or photos to a file, and everything you save can be tagged with customizable labels, and geotagged as well. That's huge if you want to keep track of when and where you saw or heard something.

Finally, I needed to tie all of the planning, ideas and goals together with project management organization. After all, what good engineer wouldn't default to project management? I didn't want a complex system that would allow me to fall into analysis paralysis, so I was overjoyed when I came across Trello. Trello combines a list-based visual planning layout with team sharing capabilities, simple but powerful tracking and notification functions, workflow automation, and the ability to update from anywhere through a smartphone app, the online platform, or by sending an email to my boards. Powerful and easy made Trello just right for me.

There you have it. Learning to live inside the perfection paradox meant learning to overcome procrastination and let things go, quitting the pursuit of better and projecting my ideal onto others, accepting failure as a good thing, and creating new habits. And now that it's done, perfectionism is cured, and good is good enough, right?

11

LETTING GOOD ENOUGH BE GOOD ENOUGH

The goal is not to be perfect by the end.
The goal is to be better today.

— Simon Sinek

G etting to good enough is a challenge in itself, but staying there makes the journey to good enough seem like a Sunday stroll in the park. Some people will argue that addiction to perfection isn't the same as an addiction to drugs or alcohol. That may be true, but one thing that is the same is the long-term struggle of a recovering addict. The ability to continue living the life you deserve requires understanding challenges will exist, and reinforcing the commitments you made to yourself when you chose to let go.

It's a lifelong challenge because perfectionists are wired that way, but isn't living the life you deserve worth the effort? Your pursuit of perfection mustn't blind you to accomplishing a worthy goal. The goal is not perfection. For some, the goal is progress; for others, the goal is excellence or success, whatever that looks like for them.

Baseball great Derek Jeter said, "I'm not perfect; no one is perfect. Everyone makes mistakes. I think you try to learn from those mistakes." Jeter should know a thing or two about that. Over his career, he batted .310, which means he got a hit in 31% of his at-bats. For that, he was paid roughly $269 million. You might ask yourself, why on earth would the New York Yankees pay that much for 31%?

Once upon a time, I might have thought the same, but that would have been the perfectionist in me looking at a 69% failure rate. Jeter may have only gotten credit for 31% of his at-bats being hits, but in reality, he was incredibly more valuable than that to the Yankees. His batting average went up several points in the playoffs, especially in the World Series. He was a stellar fielder with a nearly 98% fielder rating, winning five Gold Gloves, and was selected to 14 all-star teams. In 2020 Jeter was elected to the Baseball Hall of Fame, garnering 396 out of 397 possible votes.[24] That's pretty darn close to perfect if you ask me. The best baseball players in the world make tens of millions per year, and most fail to hit the ball as much as Jeter did.

What's the point of that story? Derek Jeter wasn't perfect, and he is considered one of the great players of the modern era (and I'm not even close to being a Yankees fan). We don't need to be perfect to be valuable either.

For one reason or another, you think you *need* to be perfect. You don't see anything good about your imperfections, but there is actually much good to be found in them. They keep us humble, which allows us to continue learning and improving. Imperfections make us relatable, accessible, relevant and immensely valuable to others. They make us human, and allow us to empower others to be human and keep moving forward.

Perfectionism isn't the same as doing your best. In reality, perfection is the enemy of excellence. Striving to do your best is about growth and healthy achievement, whereas perfectionism is more like the shield we think will protect us from getting hurt or being ridiculed. Let go of trying to be perfect. If you feel the need to be perfect, the world is a challenging and scary place because there's only one way things can go correctly, and an infinite number of ways they can go wrong. Tim Ferriss, author of New York Times #1 bestsellers *The 4-Hour Workweek*, and *Tools of Titans* understands this as well as anyone. He gave himself a quota to write two crappy pages a day.[25] This small quantity (two pages) of imperfect work resulted in five #1 bestsellers and counting.

> PERFECTIONISM ISN'T THE SAME AS DOING YOUR BEST. IN REALITY, PERFECTION IS THE ENEMY OF EXCELLENCE.

Trying to be perfect is tiring. It's the pursuit of an unattainable state, and it paralyzes you from moving forward, holding you back while everyone else moves on. Instead, when you embrace imperfection, you can be successful, happy and free. That's it. Let go of trying to be perfect. Not you, your circumstances, or the people in your life need to be perfect to acceptable.

Imperfection means accepting yourself and the situation as it is, and liking who you are while striving to do your best. Letting go of perfection lets you make mistakes. It allows you to get past the worry and fear that it won't be good enough. As a general rule, people like real because real means mistakes, flaws and imperfection. As Simon Sinek puts it, "to be authentic is to be at peace with your imperfections."

Am I completely free of perfectionism today? Not by a longshot. It's a constant challenge to let things go, but I work hard at it. Brené Brown says, "I'm like a recovering perfectionist. For me, it's one day at a time." That's exactly what I consider myself, a recovering perfectionist.

Now I understand imperfect action beats perfect inaction every time, so I set achievable goals that stretch me, but that

I know I can accomplish. I have allowed myself to be worthy and accepted there are things I am good enough at, maybe even a few in which I've become somewhat of an expert. But I now accept that I don't have to be perfect for those things to be true. I adopted a new meaning for my signature line, "good enough isn't good enough, sign your work with excellence" to mean just that—pursuit of excellence, not perfection.

Letting go of perfection and embracing imperfection allows you to become a happier person. You become free to pursue what you want to make your life successful, whether that's in your profession, your relationships, as a parent or as a person. My relationships are better than ever. I choose to fill my life with gratitude, peace, and happiness and am happier than I have ever been. Is my life perfect? Nope. But it's excellent, and that's good enough for me!

Perfection vs. Excellence
(Author Unknown)

Perfection is being right. Excellence is being willing to be wrong.
Perfection is fear. Excellence is taking a risk.
Perfection is anger and frustration. Excellence is powerful.
Perfection is control. Excellence is spontaneous.
Perfection is judgement. Excellence is accepting.
Perfection is taking. Excellence is giving.
Perfection is doubt. Excellence is confidence.
Perfection is pressure. Excellence is natural.
Perfection is the destination. Excellence is the journey.

APPENDICES

APPENDIX 1
LIVING INSIDE THE PARADOX – 7 STEPS TO CONFRONTING YOUR PERFECTIONISM

1. Take Action – Imperfect action beats perfect inaction every day

2. Pummel Procrastination – It's getting you nowhere

    a. Break up projects/assignments into small tasks

    b. Prioritize the smaller tasks

    c. Give each task a time limit or deadline

    d. Eliminate distractions

    e. Take short breaks, movement or relaxation breathing are great

    f. Celebrate each completion/accomplishment

3. Quit Pursuing "Better" – It doesn't exist

    a. Create a list of things that cause you to keep pursuing perfect

    b. Create a list of all the results those causes have provided for you

    c.   Read the lists, then "let it go" and commit to ridding your life of the causes

4.   Stop Projecting – It's ruining your relationships

    a.   Look for the positive before you issue reality checks

    b.   Apologize for past transgressions

    c.   Be grateful for contributions from others whether it was your way or not

    d.   Be vulnerable and authentic

5.   Embrace Failure, Don't Fear It – It's an opportunity to learn and grow, not who you are

    a.   Define what you are really afraid of

    b.   Define what will actually happen if you fail

    c.   Compare the two; the outcome is probably far less scary than the fear

6.   Create New Habits – The old ones weren't serving you well

    a.   Figure out what habits you need to change

    b.   Quit doing things the old way

    c.   Decide how you are going to do things from now on

    d.   Find tools that work for you to help you institutionalize the new way

    e.   Stick with them for at least two months before deciding if you need to make changes

7.   Grant Yourself Grace – If you don't allow yourself to be imperfect, none of the other steps will matter

APPENDIX 2

TRANSCRIPT OF JEFF'S 9/23/2014 COACHING CALL WITH KARY OBERBRUNNER

Me: Hi Kary. I think I'm probably not as far along as some of the others. I'm still struggling with the material and with trying to define my dream. As a result, I'm having trouble with the story shift and my GPS, because I don't know how to put the dream into some express form. It's not crystalizing for me yet.

Kary: You said that the reason you might be struggling with this is because "I'm an X." What did you say?

Me: I'm an engineer by education and experience, so by nature we analyze things far too much, and everything has to be perfect or people die. It's hard to get past that need for perfection and over analysis. I know I struggle with it.

Kary: Do you think pilots are pretty precise people?

Me: Absolutely.

Kary: I agree with you, pilots are pretty precise. I mean, if you are off a few degrees over thousands of miles you're in another city. I think you know where I'm going with this. January a few years ago, a plane takes off over Manhattan, they hit birds, full fuel tanks, they're hanging in the air. Captain Sully is at the controls. He's a very precise guy. Tower is telling him all kinds of stuff. You've got time, go here, we'll clear a runway there, but Sully feels in his gut that he doesn't have the time. So, what does he do?

Me: He determines the best place to land the plane, where he's got the best chance of saving everyone on it, and not harming others on the ground.

Kary: Yeah. And he lands where?

Me: In the Hudson.

Kary: Was that ideal?

Me: No.

Kary: No, it wasn't ideal at all. In fact, it was so unideal that people said it was a miracle. Now we know from understanding Sully's past that it wasn't a miracle, that he was a glider pilot, and that he was used to making adjustments like that. But here's the point. Sully, that day, said that today good is better than ideal. Let me ask you Jeffrey, how much grace do you give yourself with good rather than ideal? Personally?

Me: Personally? Not much. In fact, my quote that I often say is "Good enough isn't good enough." I think it comes from that I work in government, where good enough takes on a different connotation, so I use that a lot.

Kary: Let me call on one of our friends here for a minute. We are going to get back to Jeffrey in a minute because this is really good. His lights are coming on even though he may not see them yet. I see them. What has Jeffrey been telling himself, like we all do by the way, what has he been telling himself that has been preventing his breakthrough? What do you think?

Deb: Maybe "I'm not worthy."

Kary: Yeah, that could be it. We talked about the story shift, and about how we are all telling ourselves a story. Think about the story Jeff's been telling himself. Things like "I'm an engineer." Let's finish that Jeff, all the things you've told yourself after that statement. I'm an engineer, so ... List all the things that you know in your heart sabotage your success that come after that statement.

Me: I have to be perfect. I have to be professional. That image of the engineer, that I have to be analytical, I have to be serious, I have to be right. I can't be wrong because that's a bad thing. People get hurt if you're wrong.

Kary: People get hurt if you're wrong. When Sully was on the way down over Manhattan, one of the most densely populated places on the planet, and the tower is saying you've got to go to LaGuardia, and Sully said I'm going in the Hudson, he could have been wrong. Don't you think? I mean, he could have been dead wrong, and 155 people are dead. Do you think Sully said that day that good enough is good enough?

Me: Yeah.

Kary: He did, and because he said that allowed 155 people to live. We can go through history and pull out tons of examples. Military battles, inventions, movements, initiatives, police pullovers. We could go through a million examples and show that good enough was good enough. Because it meant action. What else does good enough mean at times?

Me: That it will get the job done.

Kary: Is it fair to say, and I'm picking on you but this is for 95% of us on this call. Is it fair to say that you've accepted and promoted, because what I heard you say is that in government, you gave us another story, that in government if good enough is accepted then what?

Me: Well, in engineering, good enough isn't, because if you are wrong people could be injured or die, but in government there's that myth that, well it's good enough for government work, which means it's not really as good as it could be, but it's enough to get by.

Kary: Yeah, and you detest that.

Me: Yeah, because as an engineer good enough isn't good enough. It needs to be excellent.

Kary: Let me ask you this. Is your dream job in engineering?

Me: No sir.

Kary: That's huge. So, your learning model in your day job is not the same learning model that's going to help you achieve your dream. Is that fair?

Me: Yeah, that's correct.

Kary: That's a big one. Your day job mantra will no longer serve you in your dream job. That's part of the filter holding you back. What you've said is you have a learning model that not only no longer serves you, it actually sabotages you. Do you agree?

Me: Yes.

Kary: My question is, and this is easy to say but tough to mean, my question is, are you okay, literally and sincerely, with good enough if it moves you closer to your dream?

Me: Yes, absolutely. I've got to get there.

Kary: Good. That's a big shift. You've said you are okay with that, so your dream isn't going to be ideal the first time it comes out. And that's okay, but what's probably happening is for years you've told yourself this. Tell me when the memory is that you said for the first time, or someone else told you, Jeff, good enough isn't good enough? Did you tell yourself, or did someone else tell you that?

Me: It probably came about through conversations with others, but I started using it early in my career. Honestly it started earlier than that for me though. Even as a teenager working toward Eagle Scout, working toward becoming a junior trap shooting champion. When you have to hit more birds out of 200 than anyone else on the line to become the champion then you need to be better than everyone else. So, I started putting that pressure on myself as a teenager even though I didn't associate it the same way.

Kary: For 35 years minimum you've prided yourself, disciplined yourself to say good enough isn't good enough, and you have to be perfect.

Me: Yes, absolutely.

Kary: So now you are saying you have to unlearn that. Are you ready for your homework?

Me: Yes sir.

Kary: OK, I want you get one of those little notebooks, or your iPhone with a note app, and I want you ten times every day, and this is going to be tough Jeff, I know it is, in fact, ten is too much, because I want you to be good enough and not perfect, so we're only going to give you five. OK, because good enough is good enough. Five times, every day, in the next two weeks, I want you to post on the Facebook wall, that when you have an urge to want to be ideal, want to be perfect, that you... actually, five's too much. I'm going low Jeff, I'm going three. Can you do three? I went from ten to three. Can you do three?

Me: I think I can do three.

Kary: OK, were going three. Do you see how I'm doing this? Ten was perfect, and I just gave you grace, and said three. I want three times every day from now until the next two weeks, because you spent 35 years, I mean looking at the gun, shooting the birds, Eagle Scout, I mean you've been telling yourself a story. Engineer, I heard it, I heard all this in your Facebook post, and no condemnation, but I heard it. You know, I heard I'm an Eagle Scout, I'm in government, I'm an engineer, boom-boom-boom-boom-boom story. And you said the story no longer serves you. I want you in the next two weeks, because we don't talk again for two weeks, three times a day when you feel the urge, just like I used to feel the urge to self-injure, just like somebody feels the urge to smoke a pack of cigarettes, just like somebody else feels the urge... Jeff do you know, Jeff is an ideal addict. Is this fair to say?

Me: I think so.

Kary: For the first time tonight, do you realize that you are an ideal addict?

Me: Yeah. My wife has told me that. Not in those exact words, but she's told me that.

Kary: I'll tell you what else Jeff, number one, I can relate because I went the other way, and I would punish myself through self-injury when I wasn't good enough. That's why I'm pushing you hard tonight. But number two, here's the big one Jeff, if you don't allow yourself grace, guess what? You don't allow who else grace?

Me: I don't allow myself grace?

Kary: Yeah, if you don't allow yourself grace, as a person, and you have an ideal in your head, and that's the way that you live life, and that's the way you operate, then who else can't you give grace to?

Me: Others around me, my family, my employees, whoever.

Kary: Exactly. So is it fair to say that the people that you need to make your dream happen, because we all need people, you can't get your dream in isolation, you can only get your dream in collaboration, is it fair to say, Jeff, that people have been repelled from you? Let's just take this for a moment. Does anyone naturally want to help somebody who has "Ideal" plastered across their forehead, who has incredibly high standards and ideals? What they do subconsciously when someone had ideal, I mean perfection, expected? They run. So, Jeff, not only has this learning model not served you, but it might have actually repelled people from wanting to help you.

Me: I never thought of it like that, but yeah, it probably has.

Kary: So, what does this mean Jeff?

Me: Well, I guess, if part of what I want to do is help others I can't do that if I'm pushing people away by having this level of perfection that just isn't achievable. So somewhere I've got to let go of that so that people would allow me to help.

Kary: Yep. Here's how you're going to retrain your brain. Over the next two weeks, if you're willing, you're going to allow yourself the new mantra that says good enough is good enough, and you're going to try new things. It could be the smallest little thing. What do you think is a small thing, Jeff?

What's something you haven't been willing to try, because you haven't thought you could do it perfectly?

Me: Wow. I can think of a couple big things, but I really don't want to bite one of those off in the first week or two. I don't even know. I'm lost.

Kary: I'll tell you what. This learning model, it's part of you, so it shows up wherever you go. Let's talk about Jeff at a restaurant. About how your learning model is preventing you from achieving your dream. Are you hard on waiters and waitresses?

Me: Actually, not usually, no.

Kary: Okay, then who are you hard on?

Me: Well, I'm hard on my employees.

Kary: Okay, there you go. Talk to us. When was the last time you were hard on an employee?

Me: Today.

Kary: There you go. Didn't take you long. So today what happened? Give us the quick story.

Me: Today was one of my Superintendents, and he was supposed to update our Director with a report on some repairs that were underway, and he provided the update, but it wasn't thorough enough. Oh my God (exasperated sigh).

Kary: What, why did you say that?

Me: He gave the information that the Director needed to know what he wanted, but for me it wasn't thorough enough.

Kary: What do you think the guy walked away with, under his breath, when he felt... first of all, did you yell at him?

Me: No, I don't yell. I'm pretty good about that.

Kary: Okay, we communicate with non-verbals. Did he feel your disapproval?

Me: Yeah. I mean, I told him that I wasn't happy with the quality of the work. I don't yell, but I try to correct them, and he really didn't need correction.

Kary: There you go. Joel, on Facebook, said let's see your first post tonight. You've got a whole crowd loving you here, privately of course. You just got your first one, and that's a big one. I'm talking little, like some people would say they've never driven a different away to work in fifteen years. Why, because it's not ideal, it's not the best amount of time and fuel efficiency. And I'd say guess what you're doing tomorrow; you're taking a different way. See what I'm saying, see how this is both big and small?

Me: (crying) Yeah.

Kary: What's going to happen Jeff, is you're going to blow up your mind in a good way. And you're going to say oh my gosh, wow. Then we can talk about your dream, after you readjust your learning model.

Me: Alright. Sounds like a plan.

Kary: Okay, you've got three tomorrow. And you've got people here who are going to hold you accountable for doing it.

Appendix 3
Accepting Imperfection Affirmation

Perfection is the enemy of happiness, productivity, and healthiness. I am willing to alter my expectations to enhance my life.

My ability to accept imperfection permits happiness to enter my life. **Perfection is an obstacle to happiness.** I do my best and accept the results. By avoiding the need for perfection, I am happier, and the people around me are happier too.

I get much more accomplished when I am free of the need to be perfect. The need to be perfect can trigger procrastination. It is easy for me to get started on my work each day. I use my time wisely, accepting whatever life brings. **My best is good enough.** This attitude increases my productivity.

I am more content and relaxed when I remember that perfection is a myth. Accepting the results of my efforts ensures I sleep better and enjoy my spare time more. The desire for perfection creates stress and anxiety.

When I am more accepting of others, my relationships benefit. I realize that perfection is an impossibility for others, too. I maintain reasonable standards for the people in my life, but I avoid having unreasonable expectations. **I accept others as they are.**

Today, I am doing my best and accepting the outcomes I produce. I am content when I allow others and myself to be imperfect.

APPENDIX 4
20 SELF-REFLECTION QUESTIONS FOR PERFECTIONISTS

1. Do I require perfectionism from myself or others? Why?

2. When have I allowed the desire for perfection to get in my way?

3. In what areas do I limit myself with unrealistic expectations?

4. In what ways do I strive for perfection?

5. Do I ever find myself spending forever on a task, trying to get it *just right?*

6. What has the need for perfection cost me in the past?

7. How do I respond when I make a mistake?

8. What are my goals today? Can I achieve them without being perfect?

9. What are the most important areas of my life for me to experience improvement?

10. How have my relationships been affected by expecting too much from others?

11. Do I feel I deserve to be loved, even though I'm imperfect?

12. Do I allow myself to be "under construction?"

13. Do I accept my flaws?

14. How do my imperfections make me special?

15. What good things have my imperfections brought to me?

16. How can I embrace my imperfections?

17. When have I received accolades for a job well done—even though it wasn't perfect?

18. How can letting go of perfection improve my life?

19. What will I gain by having more reasonable expectations?

20. What would my life look like if I were twice as good in every area of my life? If it took a year to accomplish, would it be worth it?

Appendix 5

ENDNOTES

1. Swider, Brian, Dana Harari, Amy P. Breidenthal, and Laurens Bujold Steed. "The Pros and Cons of Perfectionism, According to Research." *Harvard Business Review*, December 27, 2018. https://hbr. org/2018/12/the-pros-and-cons-of-perfectionis m-according-to-research.

2. Craighead, Olivia. "Beyoncé and Adele Are Perfectionists in Their Own Ways—and We Need Both Types of Role Models." *Glamour*, February 13, 2017. https://www.glamour.com/story/ beyonce-and-adele-are-perfectionists-and-we-need- both-role-models.

3. Eby, Douglas. "Actors and perfectionism" *The Creative Mind*. http://thecreativemind.net/3657/ being-a-perfectionist/.

4. Sandoiu, Ana. "How perfectionism affects your (mental) health." *MedicalNewsToday*, October 12, 2018. https://www.medicalnewstoday.com/articles/323323.

5. Curran, Thomas, and Andrew P Hill. "Perfectionism Is Increasing over Time: A Meta-Analysis of Birth

Cohort Differences from 1989 to 2016." *Psychological Bulletin* 145, no. 4 (December 28, 2017): 410–429. https://www.apa.org/pubs/journals/releases/bul-bul0000138.pdf

6. Wendell, Bryan. "Eagle Scout Class of 2019: The Numbers behind the Number." Bryan on Scouting: A Blog for BSA's Adult Leaders. *Scouting*, February 24, 2020. https://blog.scoutingmagazine.org/2020/02/24/eagle-scout-class-of-2019-the-numbers-behind-the-largest-eagle-class-ever/.

7. Rohm, Robert A. *Who Do You Think You Are Anyway?* Atlanta, GA: Personality Insights, 2012.

8. YouTube. *Oprah Interviews Michael Jackson (1993)*, August 10, 2018. https://www.youtube.com/watch?v=VFVm_3QJrEQ.

9. Vena, Jocelyn. "Michael Jackson was 'Never Satisfied' with his music, Akon says." *MTV News*, October 23, 2009. http://www.mtv.com/news/1624593/michael-jackson-was-never-satisfied-with-his-music-akon-says/.

10. Brooks, Jon. "How to Overcome Perfectionism: Life Lessons from Kubrick to Picasso." *HighExistence*. https://highexistence.com/how-to-overcome-perfectionism-with-case-studies-from-kubrick-to-picasso/.

11. Hewitt, Paul L, Gordon L Flett, and Samuel F Mikail. *Perfectionism: A Relational Approach to Conceptualization, Assessment, and Treatment*. New York, NY: The Guilford Press, 2017.

12. Pressfield, Steven. *The War of Art*. New York, NY: Black Irish Entertainment LLC, 2002.

13. Holt, Douglas. "Todd Beamer." *Los Angeles Times*, September 20, 2001. https://www.latimes.com/la-humantoll-beamer-story.html

14. Razzetti, Gustavo. "Why Good Enough is Better than Perfect." *Liberationist*. https://liberationist.org/why-good-enough-is-better-than-perfect/.

15. Tracy, Brian. *Eat That Frog!: 21 Great Ways to Stop Procrastinating and Get More Done in Less Time*. Oakland, CA: Berrett-Koehler, 2017.

16. Mackinnon, Sean P, Cassondra M. Ray, Samantha M. Firth, and Roisin M. O'Connor. "Perfectionism, negative motives for drinking, and alcohol-related problems: A 21-day diary study." *Journal of Research in Personality* 78, (February 2019): 177-188. https://www.sciencedirect.com/science/article/pii/S0092656618303726.

17. Trijicon advertisement. *American Rifleman* 168, no. 5 (May 2020): 17.

18. Fay, Scott M. *Discover Your Sweet Spot*. New York, NY: Morgan James, 2014

19. Haden, Jeff. "Shark Tank's Barbara Corcoran Says Every Exceptional Person Suffers From Self-Doubt: How to Use Imposter Syndrome to Your Advantage." *Inc.*, March 13, 2020. https://www.inc.com/jeff-haden/shark-tanks-barbara-corcoran-says-every-exceptional-person-suffers-from-self-doubt-how-you-can-use-imposter-syndrome-to-your-advantage.html.

20. Adams, R.L., "21 Famous Failures Who Refused to Give Up." *HuffPost*, September 17, 2016. https://www.huffpost.com/entry/21-famous-failures-who-refused-to-give-up_b_57da2245e4

b04fa361d991ba?guccounter=1&guce_referrer=
aHR0cHM6Ly93d3cuZ29vZ2xlLmNvbS8&guce_
referrer_sig=AQAAAGz46gCr6CE5_-z9JT5bb7
VLPNQOijPQ7BOK8s6VE5XnBb-q56fzA4Z9Dt
SJ1MRAoJ2oN8nDS2xlPYbdmmqs9mTwOsxE
abYO8kACPCMVEeDZGHK-PZC-kado7ev
1Ty8muR2dqBjub-0CtkSXoqKHp2Bum
1xaZ6iP3WpKWglS_7ZI

21. AZQuotes.com. Norman Vincent Peale. https://www.
azquotes.com/quote/1055746.

22. Malone-Kircher, Madison. "James Dyson on 5,126
Vacuums That Didn't Work— and the One That
Finally Did." *New York Magazine*, November
22, 2016. https://nymag.com/vindicated/
2016/11/james-dyson-on-5-126-vacuums-that-
didnt-work-and-1-that-did.html.

23. Sharma, Robin. *The 5 AM Club: Own Your Morning.
Elevate Your Life*. Toronto, ON: HarperCollins, 2018

24. Baseball Reference. Derek Jeter. https://www.
baseball-reference.com/players/j/jeterde01.shtml.

25. Ferris, Tim. "The Ugly New York Times Bestseller —
The Creative Process in Action." *The Tim Ferris
Show*, December 9, 2013. https://tim.blog/2013/
12/09/the-ugly-new-york-times-bestseller-the-
creative-process-in-action/.

General Reference Sources and Recommended Reading

- American Psychological Association. https://www.apa.
org/search?query=perfectionism.

- *Psychology Today*. Sussex Publishers, LLC. https://www.
psychologytoday.com/us/search?text=perfectionism.

- Brown, Brene'. *The Gifts of Imperfection: Let Go of Who You Think You're Supposed to Be and Embrace Who You Are*. Center City, MN: Hazelden, 2010.

- Brown, Brene'. *I Thought It Was Just Me (but it isn't): Making the Journey from "What Will People Think?" to "I Am Enough"*. New York, NY: Avery, 2007.

- Bluestein, Jane. *The Perfection Deception*. Deerfield Beach, FL: Health Communications, 2015.

- Leman, Kevin. *Why Your Best Is Good Enough*. Grand Rapids, MI: Revell, 2010.

- Smith, Ann W. *Overcoming Perfectionism: Finding the Key to Balance & Self-Acceptance*. Deerfield Beach, FL: Health Communications, 2013.

ACKNOWLEDGMENTS

So many have played a role in the creation of this book. Thanks first and foremost to God for providing everything I have, everything I need, and for revealing to me my new name, my secret name, Overcomer. That is who I now am!

Thank you to my wife, Sharon, who is not only my rock, but who has provided creative input and graphic design for everything I do, and who was my graphic designer, proofreader and truth-teller on this book. And to my daughters, Arielle, Kelsey, Hayley and Emily: you four are my pride and joy. Thank you for enduring, surviving, and thriving despite all I put you through. I love you all more than words can express.

If iron sharpens iron, then Martyn Wood, Russell Moore, Craig Bolze, David Samuel, and Jack Gierak are my men of steel. Thank you for encouraging and supporting me, for providing accountability, and for suffering through as early readers. Your contributions made this book so much better than it would have been. And to all who read and offered endorsements for this book—I value your support and belief in me. Thank you.

Special thanks to Daphne V. Smith for prodding, pushing and dragging me into Author Academy Elite, encouraging me to write this book, and for providing coaching, guidance and feedback along the way. I see you pointing at me—it wouldn't have happened without you. To Phillip Van Hooser for writing the foreword and being a supportive and respected role model. And to my editors, Diana James and Tina Morlock at The Guild; the team at JetLaunch for the book's interior and cover designs; Jessica Rogers of Jrogers Photography in Dayton Ohio for the author's photos; and Kary Oberbrunner and his fantastic team that form my amazing publisher, Author Academy Elite. Thank you all for making this book (and me) so much better. You are all superstars!

ABOUT THE AUTHOR

 Jeffrey A. Kramer is an author, coach, and speaker who spent nearly 35 years building better communities as an award-winning engineer and construction manager for government agencies. Jeff spent most of those years as an obsessive perfectionist, paralyzed by the idea that he wasn't good enough, aggravating others with impossible expectations, and compensating for fear of being exposed as an imposter by overachieving, collecting credentials, and moving on before anyone could find him out.

Now a recovering perfectionist who has overcome his addiction to the ideal, Jeff focuses on building people by helping them clarify their calling, overcome their obstacles, and define their direction, so they become perfectly unhackable and are encouraged, equipped and empowered to become Ascending Leaders and rise to new heights of success.

An Unhackable Transformation coach, certified by the John Maxwell Team, Igniting Souls, and as a DISC practitioner, Jeff is also an amateur photographer, avid reader, and former athlete who unapologetically cries tears of joy when the national anthem plays during the Olympic games. Jeff and his wife, Sharon, live in Arizona and share four amazing daughters.

ABOUT THE PUBLISHER

Do you have a story inside you that you need to tell? Many people do, but sadly never get that message out of their head. If you're ready to share your message with the world, Author Academy Elite might be the choice to help you write, publish and market your book the right way! Founded in 2014 by Kary Oberbrunner and David Branderhorst to help their clients, Author Academy Elite is disrupting the publishing industry with a new model that focuses on the author first.

Author Academy Elite attracts quality authors who share a mutual commitment to help each other be successful, and create vibrant businesses around their books. The Author Academy Elite team shares advice, encouragement and resources to help you throughout the process. Find out more at https://tinyurl.com/jeffreyakramer, and receive a complimentary author guidebook.

ABOUT ASCENDING LEADERS

The two greatest days in a person's life are the day they are born and the day they discover why.

The Ascending Leaders Community is a tribe of people committed to building a better world—Physical, Cultural, Social, Familial and Spiritual. People who see a need for leadership, and seek to provide it. People with integrity, character and a servant's heart, who are willing to invest in themselves in order to better serve themselves and others.

Ascending Leaders **Clarify** their calling, **Overcome** their obstacles, and **Define** their direction so they become **Perfectly Unhackable** and are encouraged, equipped and empowered to reach new heights of success.

Discover more about the Ascending Leaders Community, including Second Saturday events and the Ascending Leaders Podcast, at jeffreyakramer.com.

YOUR NEXT STEPS WITH *THE PERFECTION PARADOX*

- **Complete the Assessment**

  Discover your Perfection Profile

- **Take the Course**

  Expose your Addiction and Escape to Excellence

- **Share the Message**

  Become a Certified Perfection Paradox Coach, Speaker & Trainer

  www.perfectionparadoxbook.com

INVITE JEFF INTO YOUR BUSINESS OR ORGANIZATION

Jeffrey A. Kramer
Author – Speaker – Coach

Jeff understands how important it is to select a speaker or coach who understands your needs, the results you are looking for, and then works hard to make sure that happens for you. To experience Unhackable Transformation, invite Jeff into your business or organization today for:

- Conferences

- Workshops

- Retreats

- Team Building Experiences

Learn more and connect with Jeff at jeffreyakramer.com